T5-CWM-666

The Poet's Tongues:
Multilingualism in Literature

The Poet's Tongues:
Multilingualism in Literature

The de Carle Lectures at the University of Otago 1968

Leonard Forster

Cambridge University Press
in association with
University of Otago Press

First published 1970 in New Zealand by The University of Otago Press
and throughout the rest of the world by
the Syndics of the Cambridge University Press
Bentley House, 200 Euston Road, London N.W.1
American Branch: 32 East 57th Street, New York, N.Y.10022
Australian Branch: 296 Beaconsfield Parade, Middle Park, Victoria 3206
and 5th floor, 184 Sussex Street, Sydney, N.S.W.2000

© Leonard Forster 1970

Library of Congress Catalogue Card Number: 76-112469
ISBN: 0 521 07766 4

Printed in New Zealand by
John McIndoe Limited, Dunedin

For my son Thomas
who stood over me while I wrote
these lectures
in Dunedin

Contents

Preface

1 General Introduction

Bilingualism and multilingualism 1; Hugo von Hofmannsthal on languages as instruments 2; bilingualism and diglossia 4; different languages used for different purposes by the same speaker 4 ff; their similar use in literature 7.

2 Middle Ages and Renaissance

Use of Latin in the Middle Ages and the Renaissance 9; Luther's table talk; *In dulci jubilo* 10 ff; Mozarabic poetry in medieval Spain 12 ff; multilingual drama in Ancient India 13; multilingual films—*Kameradschaft, La grande illusion* and others 13 ff; macaronic poetry, Folengo to Godley 14 ff; choice of language determined by literary genre 16 ff; polyglot poems—*De Amico ad Amicam,* Oswald von Wolkenstein 17; appropriate languages for certain purposes 17 ff; language loyalty—Charles d'Orléans 19; Latin the vehicle of new poetic themes 19; polyglot emblem books 20; language differences afford means of stylistic variation 22; present-day Swiss advertising 22 ff.

3 Renaissance and Baroque

Polyglot publications directed at a polyglot public 26; formulation and re-formulation 27; seventeenth-century examples in poetry 27 ff; language as material 29; international poetic diction, petrarchism 29; poetic practice in an established literary language preliminary to new departures in poetry in a vernacular—Joachim du Bellay, Jan van der Noot 30 ff; G. R. Weckherlin's court poetry in English and French 35 ff; Philip von Zesen 38; P. C. Hooft and his circle 39 ff; Constantijn Huygens 41 ff; Weckherlin in England 42 ff; Milton's poetry in Italian 44 ff; European 'poésie précieuse' 47; five-finger exercises acquiring 'soul'—Peter Altenberg 48.

4 Stefan George and R. M. Rilke

Cosmopolitan culture: French and Latin in the eighteenth century 51; Goethe's verses in English and French 53; change in attitude in the nineteenth century between William Beckford's *Vathek* (1784) and Oscar Wilde's *Salomé* (1894) 54 ff; Romanticism and nationalism 55; the poet's choice of a language a declaration of allegiance 55.

Stefan George's poems in French, English, and his two invented languages 56 ff; workshop practice 58; the result less of an allegiance to French culture than of an aversion from the German literature of his day 62.

Rilke's verses in Italian 63; Russian 63 f; and French 64 ff; allegiance by itself not enough 64; similarity of his French and German poetry 65; foreign language not burdened with irrelevant associations 66 ff; allegiance to the countryside of Canton Valais 69; relaxation, not training 69.

Assessment of George's and Rilke's poetry in foreign languages 70 ff.

5 James Joyce, Dadaism, Surrealism and After

Polyglot quotation in poetry; Ezra Pound 74; T. S. Eliot and his poems in French 75 ff; mistrust of all language 76; Joyce's *Finnegans Wake* and the polyglot pun 77 ff.

Alsatians and Lorrainers before 1914 78; Yvan Goll 79 ff; writes to communicate, thinks in images independent of pre-existing language 80; Hans Arp 82; thinks in patterns, expresses them in visual as well as literary form 82; Arp and early Dada—the sound poem and the simultaneous poem 83 ff; reference to Arp in *Finnegans Wake* 84 ff.

Liberating effect of Dada: Tzara, Ionesco, Beckett, Vroman 87; invented languages—J. R. R. Tolkien 88; concrete poetry not confined to any one language 88 ff; Ernst Toch's *Geographical Fugue* 89; continuation of Dada 89; surface translation 91 ff; language used as material, as in earlier epochs before Romanticism 93; purification of poetic diction 93; Hugh MacDiarmid, *The Caledonian Antisyzygy* 93 f.

Acknowledgements

Author and publishers are grateful to the following for permission to quote from copyright material:

Dr Ernst Jandl; Madame Jean Arp-Hagenbach for Hans Arp; Hermann Luchterland Verlag, Neuwied, for Yvan Goll; Helmut Küpper Verlag vorm. Georg Bondi, Munich, for Stefan George, whose poems are quoted according to STEFAN GEORGE WERKE· Ausgabe in zwei Bänden 1958 VERLAG HELMUT KUPPER VORMALS GEORG BONDI Düsseldorf und München, with the pagination of the original collected edition in 15 volumes published by Georg Bondi Berlin 1927-1934; Luis d'Antin Van Rooten; Faber and Faber Ltd., for T. S. Eliot; Oxford University Press, for A. D. Godley; Frau Ruth Fritzsche-Rilke for poems by R. M. Rilke; Something Else Press for Bohumila Grögerová and Josef Hiršal.

Preface

These lectures deal with a subject which has interested me since my schooldays. I have touched on it in several earlier publications, but I have never so far had the opportunity to deal with it in a wider and more coherent framework, and I am grateful to the University of Otago for allowing me to try.

My first effort was an article, 'Fremdsprache und Muttersprache: zum Problem der polyglotten Dichtung in Renaissance und Barock', *Neophilologus* XLV (1961), based on a public lecture given in German in universities in Holland, Germany, Switzerland and Czechoslovakia, itself the expansion of a footnote to an earlier article. It forms the basis for sections 2 and 3 of these lectures. I had always hoped to be able to continue the story down to the present day. A series of public lectures by various scholars at the Warburg Institute of the University of London in the spring of 1967 gave me the chance of doing so in highly concentrated form in one lecture. This lecture was also given in several Canadian universities early in 1968 and will appear shortly in French in Montreal. It has been considerably expanded to form the basis of sections 4 and 5.

Neither the de Carle lectures nor their preliminary stages are the result of systematic investigation of problems of multilingualism in literature. The examples I have dealt with are desultory ones which I have come across in the course of my day-to-day work, and my personal experience of multilingual conditions has been almost exclusively Western European. I have tried to make sense of such material as has come my way, and I realise how incomplete it is. Even so, there are certain things I have had to leave out of account. I believe however that these lectures are the first survey of this particular problem that has been made, and I hope that they may prove useful to those concerned with other aspects of it.

I owe a special debt of gratitude to colleagues at the University of Otago for help in preparing the lectures, and for many other kindnesses besides, especially Professor Eric Herd, Professor R. G. Stone, Professor Kenneth Quinn and Dr N. Zissermann; to my wife, for making the index; to the staff of the Library of the University of Otago; to the University of Otago Press for its readiness to accept the work for publication; and to the Cambridge University Press for its willingness to be responsible for it outside New Zealand.

LEONARD FORSTER

Selwyn College, Cambridge, 1968

Inter eruditos cathedram habeat polyglottes

1 General Introduction

The subject I have proposed is a vast one, and I can only hope to offer a sketch—no more—of the different ways poets have used languages other than their own for poetry from the Middle Ages down to our own time.

I shall be dealing with polyglot poets and the poetry they write, which is not necessarily polyglot. In the ordinary way one calls someone polyglot who is able to express himself with ease and fluency in three or more languages; someone able to do this in two languages is called bilingual. But there is commonly a feeling that bilingual people have complete control of both of the languages they speak; that they have two mother tongues. There is often a similar nuance to the term polyglot. We talk of bilingual or polyglot societies if two or more languages are currently understood and used in them by a substantial proportion of the population. In this sense New Zealand is a bilingual country.

These terms turn out to be rather loose in application, and linguists, who have been devoting a good deal of attention to these problems in recent years, now have a rather different set of terms which is coming gradually into use among laymen too.

This last became apparent to me when I saw in Montreal, a bilingual city which is very much aware of problems of sociolinguistics, an advertisement reading: 'Make yourself bilingual, trilingual! Berlitz School'. I do not think the Berlitz School would seriously suggest that anyone is likely to become bilingual in the traditionally accepted sense by its good offices alone. The scholar's use of the word, aided by special circumstances obtaining in Canada, has come into lay use. Linguists now avoid the word 'polyglot' and prefer to use the word 'multilingual'. The linguistic problems concerning the use of more than one language are considered to be the same in principle whether two languages or more are involved. As bilingual persons and societies are more frequent than multilingual ones, linguists tend increasingly to use the term 'bilingualism' to cover 'multilingualism' as well. What the layman calls 'bilingual', linguistic scholars now call 'equilingual', and there is a strong body of opinion among them that equilingualism—equally complete control of two languages as mother tongues—is virtually impossible; any speaker will inevitably have better control of one language in certain fields than of the other. The high standard of proficiency, which the layman associates with the term 'bilingual', is no longer so significant for the scholar. An American investigator[1] has even suggested that the minimum qualification for bilingual status is the ability of the speaker to 'produce complete meaningful utterances in the other language'. Any high-school student of French or German— or indeed of Latin or Greek—could qualify as a bilingual by this minimum standard. It is this view which is behind the Berlitz School advertisement in Montreal, and indeed behind the vigorous discussion on bilingualism now proceeding in Canada[2] and in some other countries too.

The words 'bilingual', 'multilingual', or, to come back to our original term, 'polyglot', can thus be used to cover persons who have acquired some control of one or more foreign languages either at school or later in life. This is the case with many of the poets with whom I shall be dealing. The circumstance that a language is an acquired one endows it with certain advantages for the user, to which I shall return. Meanwhile it is useful to call to mind what Hugo von Hofmannsthal has to say about foreign languages:[3]

> Die Sprachen gehören zu den schönsten Dingen, die es auf der Welt gibt. Man sagt, sie sind es, die unser Dasein vom Dasein der Tiere unterscheiden. Sie sind wie wunderbare Musikinstru-

mente, die unsichtbar immerfort neben uns herschweben, damit wir uns ihrer bedienen: die Möglichkeit der unsterblichsten Gedichte schläft immerfort in ihnen, wir aber spielen auf ihnen so albern als möglich. Trotzdem ist es nicht möglich, sie ganz um ihren Klang zu bringen. Ja, wenn wir für die Schönheit der eigenen stumpf geworden sind, so hat die nächstbeste fremde einen unbeschreiblichen Zauber; wir brauchen nur unsere welken Gedanken in sie hineinzuschütten, und sie werden lebendig wie Blumen, wenn sie ins frische Wasser geworfen werden.

Languages are among the most beautiful things in the world. It is said that it is they which distinguish our existence from that of animals. They are like wonderful musical instruments which hover around us invisibly all the time for us to make use of. The potentiality for immortal poetry lies dormant in them, but we play on them as stupidly as can be. Even so, they cannot be completely deprived of their sound. Indeed, when we have grown insensitive to the beauty of our own, any foreign language has an indescribable magic; we need only cast our faded thoughts into it and they come to life again like flowers put into fresh water.

We should bear in mind Hofmannsthal's image of languages as invisible musical instruments always at hand for us to play upon them and make them sound: you have to *learn* to play a musical instrument; and then his idea that a foreign language can be something revivifying, bringing faded thoughts to life.

We are in fact all of us more polyglot than we think. Any normally educated person uses his native tongue on a variety of different levels for different purposes. These levels should be conceived of as forming not steps but a rather irregularly inclined plane like the slope of a hill. They merge into one another, so gradually that we often do not realize which level we are operating on. The levels at or near the bottom, which we use for, perhaps, vulgar abuse, are so different from those near the top, which we use for solemn occasions or technical discussion, that they are practically different languages. This may be seen when people attempt a solemn style based on the Authorised Version of the Bible; clergymen offering extempore prayers suddenly find to their embarrassment that when addressing the Deity they cannot handle the archaic second person singular accurately; that is, they have not learned the language properly. Inconsistency in maintaining stylistic levels makes a painful impression on the reader or hearer similar to that made by mistakes in gender or in the use of irregular verbs in a foreign language.

This holds for speakers who have a full range of stylistic levels available to them in their mother tongue; it is true for most educated native speakers of English or French, but it is not by any means universal. The German Swiss lives his everyday life—including the life of the intellect—in a dialect. At the higher stylistic levels he expresses himself in literary German, especially when addressing an audience, as in formal addresses, lectures, sermons, political speeches and so on. This is substantially a different language, which he has to acquire at school, but it is close enough to the dialect in which he lives his normal life for him to feel that it is a heightened and dignified form of his ordinary means of expression. For this very reason 'many Swiss find it easier to make conversation in French or English than in Standard German, because they have no practice in using Standard German in everyday speech'.[4] The Swiss lives in a state of what linguists have called 'diglossia', in which 'two varieties of a language exist side by side throughout the community, with each having a definite role to play'.[5] This state of affairs is fairly common, especially in the Arab world, and it presents certain parallels with the position of Latin in the Romance-speaking countries in the Middle Ages, which persisted in Italy much later still. But there are plenty of German-speaking Alsatians, Lorrainers and Luxemburgers who are similarly placed but for whom the higher stylistic levels are accessible not in German but in French. This state of affairs seems entirely natural to them; the two languages have perfectly distinct functions in their lives, though these functions may often overlap. Many Welshmen find themselves in a similar situation, and I suppose also many Maoris, and there are of course countless parallels elsewhere, especially in Eastern Europe and in the Orient. These are organically bilingual or multilingual communities, in which the functions of the different languages are clearly understood and play a natural part in people's lives.

An American scholar describes conditions in rural India as follows[6]: 'One form of the sub-regional dialect is used with traders from nearby bazaar towns. Other different forms may be employed with wandering performers or religious ascetics. There is some evidence to show that in earlier times two or three different sub-regional literary dialects cultivated by different groups of literati co-existed in the region. Thus, wandering ascetics of the Krishna cult might use Braj Bhasa, while worshippers of Ram would use Aradhi. Standard Hindi is the norm for intercourse with educated outsiders. We also found it used in certain religious caste or village uplift meetings. On other occasions, especially in business transactions or when talking to educated Muslims, Urdu is called for. Furthermore, a few of the more educated people know English and there are others who have at least some knowledge of Sanskrit. These two languages, though not directly related to the local forms, function as integral parts of the village stylistic web. Educated speakers tend to switch freely from one language to another when conversing about urban subjects, often inserting entire English phrases into their Hindi discourse [. . .]. Sanskrit is an essential component of certain Brahminical communication roles.'

There is an interesting West African writer, Chinua Achebe, who writes novels in English about his own people in Nigeria. The linguistic situation which emerges from these novels is as follows. First there are the various tribal vernaculars, which everyone speaks, but which are mostly not mutually intelligible. Then there is Pidgin as an intertribal vehicle of communication. Above this there is English, used on solemn occasions and among intellectuals.[7]

These are conditions of which I have no personal knowledge, but they can be paralleled in various European communities. I remember in the late thirties having a couple of hours to wait between trains in the Alsatian city of Mulhouse. I spent the time in a café near the station. At the next table were three worthy middle-aged petit-bourgeois citizens of the place, discussing things in general over their beer. Their conversation was largely concerned with their families and friends. They were speaking Alsatian —a German dialect. Soon they started talking about local politics and the French technical terms—*mairie, préfecture, conseil*— began inevitably to creep in. With a shift to national—i.e. French —politics, about which they were naturally informed almost exclusively through French-language radio and press, the proportion of French increased, and by the time they had got on to international politics the conversation was being conducted entirely in French. There was no indication that they were conscious of any change having taken place; they were simply using perfectly natural means of expression suited to the circumstances. All these cases fall under the heading of what has come to be known as 'languages in contact' since Uriel Weinreich's pioneer work of that title in 1953.[8]

For people like myself and many others, who grew up in one language and acquired reasonable control of one or more foreign languages later, a similar—though not by any means identical—state of affairs often holds true. One tends to reserve certain languages for certain purposes; one is more at home in dealing with certain subjects in one language than in another; one may conduct one's emotional life in one, one's intellectual life in another, and do the shopping in a third. This is in fact what I was doing earlier this year in the bilingual city of Montreal: I lived my family life in English; I did my teaching as Visiting Professor of German at McGill University entirely in German, as the tradition of the place required; and I did my shopping largely in French. A good deal earlier in my life I found myself involved in a similar linguistic specialization. The accidents of modern language study at school and university had brought it about that by the time I took my degree in modern languages at Cambridge I was virtually unable to maintain an intelligent conversation about literature with my contemporaries who were studying English, because the critical vocabulary I had learned to use was mainly German and I knew of no English equivalents—in a good many cases there weren't any. Moreover, a student brought up, as I was, on Scherer, Gundolf, Korff, and Fritz Strich had few critical concepts in common with a pupil of F. R. Leavis, and in more senses than one we were not speaking the same language. Without fully realizing it, and without being in any sense equilingual, I was living an important part of my intellectual life in German.

At this stage it is worth looking at some statistics. It has recently been pointed out that there are about thirty times as many languages in the world as there are countries to house them.[9] This means that a large proportion of the world's population is necessarily bilingual to a certain degree. This is a situation which most native speakers of English do not normally have to face, though it is in fact common enough in the British Isles—in Wales and the Scottish Highlands—and even here in New Zealand. Even so, it is very easy for English speakers never to come in contact with it. A Dutch colleague in New Zealand told me a short time ago of an experience his wife (also Dutch) had had. She was visiting with friends, native-born New Zealanders, and at some point had occasion to speak to her husband on the telephone. Naturally, she spoke to him in Dutch. When she had finished, her hosts—mother and daughter, aged about sixty and thirty-five respectively—confessed that this was the first time in their lives that they had ever heard a foreign language spoken. Native speakers of English are fortunate; there are 266 million of them. Speakers of other languages—e.g. Dutch—are less favourably placed. The spread of communications and the pressure of the mass media, which naturally operate with the major languages, are forcing more and more people into bilingualism. Indeed, as W. F. Mackey points out, we may even look forward to a state of affairs in which, on a world scale, there will be more bilinguals than unilinguals.

Against the background I have sketched the idea of polyglot poets should seem rather less strange than it may well have done at first. Since the Romantics we have all been brought up to believe that each language has its mystery and its soul, and that these are very sacred things, in whose name indeed much blood has been shed in our own lifetime and is still being shed. I am not for the moment concerned with the origin of this belief or with its justification. I want to make the point that, if we put sentiment aside, there are very many people and very many situations for which different languages are simply tools appropriate to certain definite purposes, analogous to the different stylistic levels within any one language.

1. The quotation is from Einar Haugen, *The Norwegian Language in America: a Study in Bilingual Behavior*, Philadelphia 1953, I, p. 7. See also his *Bilingualism in the Americas*, Alabama 1956. The following works give useful information and bibliography: Veroboj Vildomec, *Multilingualism*, Leiden 1963; Dell Hymes, ed., *Language in Culture and Society—a Reader in Linguistics and Anthropology*, New York 1964; *Colloque sur le multilinguisme Brazzaville 1962*, Conseil Scientifique pour l'Afrique, Publication 87, Lagos-Nairobi-London 1964; Nels Anderson, ed., *Studies in Multilingualism* (= *International Studies in Sociology and Social Anthropology* VIII), Leiden, 1969; M. Béziers and M. van Overbeke, *Le bilinguisme*, Louvain 1968; William Bright, ed., *Sociolinguistics: Proceedings of the UCLA Sociolinguistics Conference 1964*, The Hague 1966; Joshua A. Fishman, ed., *Readings in the Sociology of Language*, The Hague 1968, contains an interesting series of papers on problems of multilingualism, pp. 473-584. See also Norman Denison, 'Sauris: a Trilingual Community', *Man* III (1968), pp. 578 ff.
2. See *A Preliminary Report of the Royal Commission on Bilingualism and Biculturalism*, Ottawa 1965 and *Report of the Royal Commission on Bilingualism and Biculturalism I, The Official Languages*, Ottawa 1967.
3. Hugo von Hofmannsthal, 'Französische Redensarten', *Die prosaischen Schriften gesammelt*, Berlin 1907, II, p. 105.

4. Hans Kuhn, *Language and Nation*, Australian National University, Canberra 1965, p. 14.
5. Charles A. Ferguson, 'Diglossia' in Hymes, op. cit., p. 429 ff., previously in *Word* XV (1959) pp. 325 ff.
6. John J. Gumperz, 'Speech Variation and the Study of Indian Civilisation' in Hymes, op. cit., p. 420; previously in *American Anthropologist* LXIII (1961) pp. 976-988.
7. Especially his *A Man of the People*, London 1966. See also John Spencer, ed., *Language in Africa*, Cambridge 1963.
8. Uriel Weinreich, *Languages in Contact*, 2nd ed., The Hague 1963, a classic work to which I am much indebted in what follows.
9. W. F. Mackey, *Bilingualism as a World Problem*, Montreal 1967, p. 13 ff. See also Anthony Sampson, *The New Europeans*, London 1968, esp. chapter 14.

2 Middle Ages and Renaissance

This is the way languages were regarded in the Middle Ages and the Renaissance. In those days educated people spoke and wrote Latin with an uncomplicated matter-of-factness which most of us nowadays only achieve in our mother-tongue. There was a wide range of subjects for which no other vehicle existed: it was the international language for instance of scientific and philosophical thought. A Welshman who has an important contribution to make to nuclear physics nowadays makes it in English, because Welsh lacks the terminology. In an analogous case in the Middle Ages both the Welshman and the Englishman would have done it in Latin, for the same reason. At a certain conceptual and stylistic level Latin was the natural vehicle for what they had to say. G. G. Coulton devoted the greater part of one of his many books[1] to proving, with chapter and verse, that medieval clerics did not really know any Latin—by the standards of a classical scholar brought up in the nineteenth-century tradition. Even if he were right, it still would not affect the fact that they used such Latin as they knew as an efficient means of communication for dealing with matters of considerable intellectual complexity. The conversation of Martin Luther was recorded by his table-companions. They all conversed in German, but it is noticeable that when discussing the things of the mind, and especially theological matters, Luther switched freely from German to Latin, often including whole Latin phrases or sentences in his German discourse. This circumstance has been the subject of an interesting study by a Swedish scholar, Birgit Stolt, who tries *inter alia* to determine whether it reflects the usage of Luther himself or of the friends who took down what he said. For our purposes this question is immaterial; what the record in effect presents is the speech habits of a closely knit circle of learned men,[2] one of whose main concerns was the presentation of Christian doctrine in a new light to the German people in German. It was in this group that Luther's great translation of the Bible into German took shape, which had a decisive influence on the development of the German language. They were therefore people who were abnormally conscious of the importance of the vernacular, yet their conversation among themselves about matters which lay very close to their hearts was bilingual.

It is thus not surprising to find bilingual or multilingual verses being written. By this I mean verses written in two or more different languages. There are in fact many medieval poems preserved which are written in alternate lines or half-lines of Latin and vernacular. The professional Germanist here thinks at once of the Old High German *De Heinrico,* but a more generally familiar example is the fifteenth-century German Christmas carol *In dulci jubilo*:[3]

> *In dulci jubilo*
>   Nun singet und seid froh!
>   Unsers Herzens Wonne
> *Leit in praesepio*
>   Und leuchtet vor die Sonne
> *Matris in gremio.*
> *Alpha es et O!*
>
> *O Jesu parvule,*
>   Nach dir ist mir so weh,
>   Tröst mir mein Gemüte,
> *O puer optime,*
>   Durch aller Jungfraun Güte,
> *O princeps gloriae!*
> *Trahe me post te!*

>*Ubi sunt gaudia?*
>Niendert mehr denn da,
>Da die Engel singen
>*Nova cantica*
>Und die Schellen klingen
>*In Regis curia.*
>Eia wärn wir da!
>
>*Mater et filia*
>Ist Jungfrau Maria.
>Wir waren gar verdorben
>*Per nostra crimina;*
>Nu hat sie uns erworben
>*Coelorum gaudia!*
>*Quanta gratia!*

The four stanzas of the carol are built to the same pattern: lines 1, 4, 6 and 7 are in Latin, 2, 3 and 5 are in German, though there is some slight variation in stanzas 1 and 3. The rhyme-scheme is *aaba baa*. Thus the second line of the stanza, which is always in German, rhymes with the first, which is always in Latin. This indicates a close association of the two languages in the mind of the writer. But we can go further. The sentences throughout the poem consist of phrases from both languages. The last line of each stanza, which is an exclamation or invocation standing by itself, is an exception, and this is in accordance with the music, which requires the last line to be repeated and thus to have independent value as a syntactical unit. We may sum up by saying that the text shows close integration of the two languages, which must have been valid for the writer, the singers and the audience. This is not a learned poem but a popular one, which appeals to a large public, not necessarily highly educated, but obviously bilingual in the technical sense.

This is a phenomenon easily occurring in conditions of bilingualism. It is even more likely to occur in conditions of diglossia. There is a Swiss-German nursery rhyme, familiar to parents taking unwilling children out for a walk, which goes as follows:

>Eins zwei drei
>Lupfet euri Bai
>Lupfet euri Bai Bai Bai
>Dass mir kömme hai hai hai.

One two three, shift your legs, shift your legs legs legs, so that we get home home home.

Now there is no Swiss dialect in which *drei* can rhyme with the equivalent form to Standard German *Bein* (leg), which in its turn however in nearly all Swiss dialects gives a good rhyme to the equivalent form to Standard German *Heim* (home).[4] The rhyme is only possible if the words 'Eins zwei drei' are taken as Standard German. The rest of the poem is in Swiss German. Here, on a minute scale, we have a similar case of a bilingual poem, and here too on the popular, not on the learned level.

Moslem Southern Spain in the eleventh to the thirteenth centuries developed a highly sophisticated civilization in which the languages of culture were Arabic and to a lesser extent Hebrew. Many Jewish poets for instance wrote both in Hebrew and in Arabic. In both languages a kind of poem was cultivated called *muwaššaha*, which had a coda at the end called *harǧa*. Many of these poems seemed to 'go off' into incomprehensible nonsense in the *harǧa*. One of the most exciting events in medieval studies in the last thirty years was the discovery by an Oxford scholar, the late S. M. Stern,[5] in 1948 that these incomprehensible passages made sense if they were taken not as corrupt Hebrew or Arabic but as archaic Spanish. Stern recovered in this way a respectable corpus of the earliest lyric poetry in any Romance language. What some of the complete poems now show us is a conventional situation in which a poet expresses his longing for a beautiful slave-girl in the language of culture, whereupon in the coda the girl replies in the language of the people. Both interlocutors are deemed to understand both languages, and so of course is the public for which these poems were designed. This literary use of what was otherwise a non-literary language doubtless imparted a certain piquancy to the poem, parallel perhaps to that produced by Bernard Shaw in a diglossic, not bilingual, situation in *Pygmalion*.

There are also poems written in alternate stanzas of different vernaculars, especially if they are in dialogue. An example of this is a well-known pastourelle by the Provençal poet Raimbaut de Vaqueiras in which a minstrel attempts—unsuccessfully—to seduce the wife of a Genoese burgher.[6] The minstrel speaks Provençal, the woman speaks Italian. The two dialects are deemed to be mutually comprehensible to the speakers—and of course to the poet's audience. They serve the purpose of neat characterization. There is a similar example in nineteenth-century Flanders, in which a townsman makes advances to a country girl: he speaks French, she speaks Flemish; he too is unsuccessful; each has no difficulty in understanding the other. Despite the rejected towns-man's final stanza, which begins with the words 'Va-t'en donc, futile Flamande', the audience at which this song is aimed is clearly Flemish, but familiar with French.[7] The use of different languages or dialects for characterization is of course very com-mon on the stage. Highly sophisticated cases are to be found in early Indian drama, notably in Kalidasa's play *Sakuntala* which Goethe admired so much. Here the high-ranking characters speak Sanskrit, the others a variety of different Prakrits.[8] The linguistic conditions reflected are analogous to those obtaining in rural India at the present time which I have already mentioned. This device is seldom used nowadays except in comedy, where the difference of language gives rise to amusing misunderstandings, as in Tristan Bernard's *L'anglais tel qu'on le parle* (1899), in which the central character is an Englishman who cannot speak French. Its occurrence in serious drama is extremely restricted, though there is of course Shakespeare's use of French in *Henry V* and Carl Zuckmayer's use of English in his play about atomic spies *Das kalte Licht* (1955). Polyglot writing of this kind presup-poses a polyglot audience. The situation is rather different in the film, because of the possibility of using sub-titles in which the un-familiar language or languages can be translated without interfering with the action on the screen. Less use has been made of this medium than one might think; the convention of live theatre has been too strong. In the nineteen-thirties there were three notable films which exploited the contrast of languages—G. W. Pabst's *Kameradschaft,* Jean Renoir's *La grande illusion,* and one of the few good Nazi films, *Friesennot.*[9] *Kameradschaft* deals with a mining disaster in Lorraine, where the newly drawn post-World War I frontier runs straight across the galleries of the mine; the explosion occurs on the French side, and the German miners break down the steel bars across the gallery and rescue their French mates. The Germans speak German, the Frenchmen French, and in the scenes above ground on either side of the frontier the normal languages are used. The message of the film is the triumph of common humanity represented by the working class over the artificial barriers of nationality, and this is brought out effectively by the contrast of languages. Part of *La grande illusion* takes place in a German prisoner of war camp in World War I. Here too class solidarity is shown overcoming national barriers in wartime, but it is not the workers. The aristocratic French officer and the aristocratic German camp commandant

have common ground, and this is expressed in the circumstance
that the language they sometimes speak with one another, when
they are closest to one another, is English—the language of the
race-track and the hunting-field. *Friesennot* shows the fate of a
small German language-island buried in the forests of Russia and
forgotten by the world. After the Revolution it is discovered by an
aircraft, and a Russian patrol is sent to investigate; the Russians
speak Russian and there are no subtitles. This emphasized for the
German film audience the total strangeness of Russian civilization,
and the language was used with skill and restraint. The polyglot
film is capable of considerable development.[10]

An extreme example of the blending of two languages in poetry
is the so-called macaronic verse, of which the most famous practi-
tioner was the sixteenth century Italian Teofilo Folengo.[11] He
devised an idiom on a Latin basis consisting mainly of Latinized
Italian words with Latin inflexional endings, Latin syntax and
Latin scansion. Folengo, in his time and place, was operating in a
situation of diglossia, with Latin as the higher language and
Italian as the lower. The grotesquely humorous effect of his work
arises precisely from the discrepancy between these two forms
and the incongruous way they are combined. Speaking of young
spendthrifts, Folengo observes in book VII of his comic epic
Maccaronea (1517):

> ... Postquam giocarunt nummos, tascasque vodarunt,
> Postquam pane caret cophinum, coelaria vino,
> In fratris properant, datur his extemplo cappuzzus.

When they have gambled away their money and emptied their
pockets, when there is no more bread in the basket and no
more wine in the cellar, they hurry off to the monastery where
they at once assume the habit.

He was rapidly imitated in other countries,[12] especially Germany,
where the gap between the two languages corresponded to a
situation of bilingualism, not of diglossia. The incongruity is thus
increased, but the resultant products necessarily had a much
narrower appeal and were much less deeply rooted in the cultural
life of the community than Folengo's were. The most familiar
example is probably the ballet at the end of Molière's *Le Malade
imaginaire,* showing an oral examination for the degree of Doctor
of Medicine; the candidate passes with honours by answering
every question with the words: 'Clysterium donare, Postea seignare, Ensuitta purgare':

Quartus Doctor: De hiero maladus unus
Tombavit in meas manus:
Habet grandam fievram cum redoublamentis,
Grandam dolorem capitis,
Et grandum malum au côté,
Cum granda difficultate
Et pena de respirare:
Veillas mihi dire,
Docte Bacheliere,
Quid illi facere?
Bachelierus: Clysterium donare,
Postea seignare,
Ensuitta purgare.

Macaronics retained a certain vogue as academic diversion all over Europe until our own century. A. D. Godley's well-known lines on the motor bus,[13] written in 1914, show the final stage of this particular linguistic form of playing with culture; while practising it, he is also in a quiet way poking fun at it. His recipe is very simple and is an essentially macaronic one; he sees that the words *motor* and *bus* could structurally be Latin words (and *motor* of course *is* a Latin word); he proceeds to decline them according to their respective declensions, and then to build a little poem round the result, which embodies Latin, pseudo-Latin and un-Latinized English in a way which goes beyond the macaronic conventions devised by Folengo. English and Latin syntax are combined in much the same way as we saw done in *In dulci jubilo,* but what there was organic and natural here derives its effect from the circumstance that it is unnatural, not reflecting the way in which anyone in early twentieth-century Oxford thought or spoke, and therefore comic. The mention of the names of Oxford streets ties it down to a particular locality and marks it for what it is— a very accomplished donnish joke with a limited, though quite genuine, appeal. It is a far cry from *In dulci jubilo.*

What is this that roareth thus?
Can it be a Motor Bus?
Yes, the smell and hideous hum
Indicat Motorem Bum!
Implet in the Corn and High
Terror me Motoris Bi;
Bo Motori clamitabo
Ne Motore caedar a Bo—
Dative be or Ablative,
So thou only let us live;—

Whither shall thy victims flee?
Spare us, spare us, Motor Be!
Thus I sang, and still anigh
Came in hordes Motores Bi,
Et complebat omne forum
Copia Motorum Borum.
How shall wretches live like us,
Cincti Bis Motoribus?
Domine defende nos
Contra hos Motores Bos.

In medieval literature, as H. J. Chaytor pointed out, there was 'a convention which laid down that the choice of language was determined by the literary genre in question, not by the nationality of the author.'[14] The North Italian troubadours from the thirteenth to the fifteenth centuries wrote lyric poetry in Provençal and narrative poetry in French; Italian tended to be restricted to legal prose. Ramon Vidal de Besalú at the end of the twelfth century declared that French was best suited to certain poetic genres—romanz, retronsas and pasturellas—, while Provençal was more appropriate to others—vers, cansos and sirventes. He does not consider his own native language, Catalan, at all in this connexion. In the thirteenth century King Alfonso of Castile, whose native language was Castilian Spanish, wrote his lyric poetry in Galician-Portuguese, which at that time was regarded as the proper medium for lyric poetry in the northern part of the Hispanic peninsula (in the southern part, as we saw, the proper media were Arabic and Hebrew). This is the Romance world. In the Germanic world the dialects of the Low Countries were at first the fashionable languages for courtly literature; the knight Henric van Veldeke, writing in the Dutch dialect of his native Limburg, inaugurated a new style of courtly literature in Germany, where for some considerable time an affectation of Flemish speech was well looked on in certain circles, and the Germans even had a special word for it—vlaemen. Later the language of poetry in Flanders was made to approximate to High German. In England, where the two cultures met, the English, supposedly not greatly gifted for foreign languages, wrote in Anglo-Norman and Latin besides English, and Gower and Lydgate wrote in all three. A fifteenth century manuscript in the Cambridge University Library contains a charming polyglot poem in English, Anglo-Norman and Latin, deemed to be addressed by a young man to a young woman, and her reply in the same form, entitled respectively De amico ad *amicam* and *Responcio*.[15] This is not merely a *tour de force* by a talented linguist; it presupposes a polyglot audience in England capable of appreciating it, and does not stand alone.

De Amico ad Amicam

A celuy que pluys eyme en mounde,
Of alle tho that I have found,
 Carissima,
Saluz od treyé amour,
With grace and joye and alle honour,
 Dulcissima
Sachez bien, pleysant et beele,
That I am right in good heele,
 Laus Christo!
Et moun amour donné vous ay,
And also thine owene night and day
 In cisto.
Ma tresduce et tresamé,
Night and day for love of thee
 Suspiro.
Soyez permenant et leal;
Love me so that I it feele,
 Requiro [...]

It is a very different case from the famous set piece by the Austrian minnesinger Oswald von Wolkenstein (1367-1445), in which he introduces six languages.[16] That is just blatant showing off by a genial extrovert, proud of his (rather dubious) multilingual accomplishments, strutting about and inflating his chest in front of a (hypothetical) lady. The combination of languages he displays is not functional in the sense that it reflects an actual multilingual situation in a given community, nor in the sense that he uses certain languages for certain literary ends. It is purely personal.

The idea that certain languages were specially proper for specific purposes lasted into the sixteenth century when Charles V, King of Spain, Emperor of Germany, and Duke of Burgundy, maintained, so it is said, that French was the language to speak with one's ambassadors, Italian with one's women, German with one's stable boys (according to another version, with one's horse) and Spanish with God.[17] His contemporary Margaret of Navarre asserted rather differently in the *Heptaméron* that 'le langage castillan est sans comparaison mieux déclarant cette passion d'amour que n'est le françois';[18] in other words, Spanish is the language of love. Three hundred years later the Austrian dramatist Franz Grillparzer was of the same opinion when he set up the following canon:[19]

> Zum Singen ist die italienische Sprache,
> etwas zu sagen: die deutsche,
> darzustellen: die griechische,
> zu reden: die lateinische,
> zu schwatzen: die französische,
> für Verliebte: die spanische
> und für Grobiane: die englische.

Italian is the language for singing; German if you have something to say; Greek for demonstration; Latin for oratory; French for gossip; Spanish for lovers; and English for louts. But Grillparzer is not prescribing the use of these various languages for specific purposes: he is thinking of their spirit or 'soul' in a post-Romantic sense. Even so, in our own day there are conventions in these matters; for the past forty years, in fact since Hollywood rose to dominance in the film world at the end of World War I, and the impact of American jazz music at much the same time, the obligatory language of love for (probably) the greater part of the inhabitants of Britain has not been English at all, but American. The circumstance that this is now no longer true to the same extent is largely due to the Beatles.

The question of how poets in the Middle Ages and the Renaissance obtained their knowledge of languages and what their degree of proficiency was, is one which I must perforce leave unexamined. For my purpose it is sufficient to note the fact that certain languages were used in certain combinations in certain ways. The question of proficiency is always a difficult one to solve on written evidence alone, and how difficult it can be when confronted face to face may be illustrated by an anecdote. G. W. von Zedlitz, the first Professor of Modern Languages at what is now the Victoria University of Wellington, was the offspring of a German father and an English mother. He went to school first in Germany and then in England and he took his degree at Oxford. Much of his early life was spent in very polyglot environments in Switzerland, Italy and the Riviera. The story is told of him as a young man that he was at a tea-party somewhere on the continent where he 'noticed a tall fine-looking man who spoke English as well as I did; and I at once put him down as an

Englishman. Then a few minutes later I heard him speaking French and thought he must, after all, be a Frenchman. But when he began to speak German I *knew* he was a Russian.'[20]

It is clear that people in earlier centuries had a much less developed sense of what linguists have come to call 'language loyalty'[21] than most of us have today. This is apparent even in situations which we would nowadays consider extreme. In the fifteenth century the French general Charles d'Orléans was captured by the hated English and spent twenty-five years in an English prison. He was a reputable poet in French and passed the time of his long imprisonment in learning English and even writing a number of delightful poems in English, which are still preserved.[22] English was the language of the enemy. The difference in attitude becomes apparent if we try to envisage a parallel case in our own day, for instance a German general in Russian captivity. Though plenty of German generals were captured by the Russians in World War II and kept prisoners for as much as eight or ten years, it is hard to imagine any of them trying his hand at writing poetry in Russian, or feeling the slightest inclination to do so, for language loyalty would restrain him.

The current literary use by a poet of a language not his own, or of a variety of different languages, was only possible because poetry operated with a relatively restricted range of subject matter, formulae and topoi, which were international and formed part of a general European cultural heritage. This remained true in the Renaissance and the seventeenth century, when most poets wrote their first verses not in their mother tongue, but in Latin, at school. Latin was not a mother tongue for anyone; all those who used it had to learn it. In one sense therefore the whole vast Latin literature of the Middle Ages and the Renaissance is polyglot poetry, and ought to be considered here from that point of view. It would indeed be an interesting task to examine the effect on Latin writing of the various vernacular traditions of the authors, the effect on grammar and syntax, vocabulary and style, and even on subject-matter.[23] This would be an enormous undertaking, and all I can do here is to call attention to it and pass on. The opposite case, the effect of Latin on the vernaculars, has been much more intensively studied.

It is precisely because Latin was the international second language that the common European heritage of poetic themes and formulae is most clearly recognizable in its literature. They appear first in Latin and then later in the vernacular literatures,

and since the great work of Ernst Robert Curtius broke new
ground this aspect has received a good deal of attention.

It is in the emblem that this stock of formulae is most easily
seen, and here too Latin leads the way. 'Emblem' is a technical
term which designates a combination of pictures, motto and
poem.[24] The motto and the poem elaborate and interpret the
picture. The first person to produce emblems in this sense was
the Italian jurist Andrea Alciati in the sixteenth century, whose
book *Emblemata* first appeared in Latin at Augsburg in 1531
and went through countless editions. He began with allegorical
interpretation of the coats of arms and mottoes of his patrons or
prospective patrons, and then proceeded to treat accepted common-
places in the same way. Much of his material was drawn from the
Greek Anthology and the works on history and natural history
handed down from classical antiquity, especially Pliny. For instance, his emblem 73 shows a naked blindfolded Cupid in the
act of breaking a thunderbolt; the motto is 'Vis amoris', the
power of love, and the poem is a short epigram:

> Aligerum fulmen fregit Deus aliger, igne
> Dum demonstrat uti fortior ignis amor,

pointing out that love is stronger than fire. Here the poem only
consists of a single distich, but Alciati had no rule about length,
and some of the verses to his emblems contain as many as 30 or
40 lines. The use of the international language assured his book
a wide circulation, and the pictures stimulated translation and
imitation. The genre was rapidly taken over into the various
vernacular languages and the polyglot emblem book becomes one
of the characteristic literary products of the sixteenth and seventeenth centuries. Enterprising publishers caused popular emblem
books to be translated, but the original text (especially if it was
in Latin) was often retained alongside the translation, and there
are cases in which the texts to the emblem are the work of one
author writing in different languages. The best example known to
me is the work of the Dutch poet Jacob Cats (1577-1660), *Silenus
Alcibiadis sive Proteus,* also known under the title of one of its
parts, *Sinn- en Minnebeelden* (Middelburg 1618), a piece of most
elaborate artistry. Each of the beautifully engraved pictures is
interpreted from three different points of view, *amatorium, morale*
and *sacrum,* applicable to love, everyday morals, and religion—
and at the same time to youth, maturity and age, in the sense that
youth is the time for love, maturity for sound conduct and age for

religion. Each of these three aspects is treated in three languages—
Latin, French and Dutch; as far as can be established, Cats himself is responsible for all three. What this book offers is quite
simply the formulation of the same thought in three different
languages. A certain degree of variation is assured by the circumstance that Cats, unlike Alciati, writes the same number of lines
to illustrate each picture, and that the different languages are
not treated alike; in Latin and Dutch he works with eight lines
and in French with only four. The French version is thus shorter
and sometimes places the emphasis on different aspects of the
subject.

Cats's emblem-book is a good example of the way poets in the
seventeenth century liked to consider a theme from different and
often contrary points of view. For instance, the tortoise is conceived of as carrying the burden of its shell about with it. This
can be allegorized under the heading *morale* as the intellectual
and moral qualities which are part of our make-up, as the shell
is of the tortoise; under the heading *sacrum* however the shell
becomes the burden of sin; and as *amatorium* it becomes the
pain of love which the lover carries around with him and cannot
escape from, however far he flees. In considerations of this kind
the different languages have no specific part to play; they are
just vehicles, and one language is as good as another for expressing the allegorical concepts—whether Dutch, French or Latin.
And so it is not surprising that almost none of the congratulatory
poems at the beginning of the book mention the use of three
languages in it. The two exceptions are interesting; one is by
Daniel Heinsius, the great scholar, who was equally famous for
his poems in Latin, Greek and Dutch and who therefore appreciated the polyglot character of Cats's book; the other is by a
foreigner, Joshua Sylvester, the translator of Du Bartas's religious
epic *La Semaine* into English. He lived in Middelburg in Zealand
as the agent of the Merchant Adventurers' Company of London,
and was thus alive to the use of foreign languages. As though to
demonstrate this, the sonnet in which he praises the 'Trilingue
stile' of the poet Cats is written in French.[25]

In other multilingual emblem books the languages are treated
rather more freely; they are used to illustrate different aspects
of the emblem. The Dutchman Otto Vaenius produced a Latin
work, *Quinti Horatii Flacci Emblemata* (Antwerp 1607), in which
that gifted engraver illustrated, emblematized and allegorized passages from Horace. In later editions (*e.g.* Brussels 1683) verses

in Italian, Dutch and French (and, in a later edition still, German)
were added, each of which interpret Horace's original remark
slightly differently, or concentrate on different features of the
emblematic engraving. So for instance the emblem illustrating
the Horatian tag 'In medio constitit virtus' shows in the foreground
three allegorical figures: Virtue standing in the centre between
Avarice, with a bulging sack of gold, and Extravagance, who is
carelessly throwing money away. In the background can be seen
the sun, with Icarus falling from the sky because he flew too high,
while Daedalus, rather lower down, remains airborne. The Dutch
verses do not mention Daedalus and Icarus and restrict themselves to praising Virtue in the sense of a canny prudence in money
matters; the Italian and French verses both mention Icarus, but
treat him quite differently. The various languages are here used
as means of variation, but the variation has nothing specific to
do with the language chosen. For instance, nothing is said in the
Italian verses which could not equally well be said in French or
Dutch, and *vice versa*. Nothing important would be lost if the
languages were switched round while the subject matter remained
the same. The circumstance that Dutch readers were evidently
expected to be particularly interested in money squares to some
extent with the English jibe that:

> In matters of commerce the fault of the Dutch
> Is giving too little and asking too much,

but no one would seriously wish to suggest that the Italians and
French were not equally money-conscious, particularly as the
Italians still retained their importance as international financiers,
closely rivalled at this time by the French Huguenots. The circumstance that different languages are used as variations in itself
presupposes that many readers of the book would be expected
to be able to appreciate one or more of the variations. Similar
cases may be found in our own day, though on quite a different
level. Some time ago I came across a beer-mat in Switzerland,
advertising a brand of non-alcoholic beer called 'Ex!' in the
three official languages of the country. The letterpress read:

> Ex! Beliebt bei Erwachsenen und Kindern. Gut gekühlt
> trinken!
> Ex! Mousse et pétille comme la bière. Nourrit et désaltère!
> Ex! La bibita che nutre e disseta. Si conserva lungamente.

If one assumed that the three texts were drafted in accordance
with the results of market research among the three sections of

the community, one would be led to draw certain conclusions from the circumstance that German Swiss do not get told that this drink is nourishing and thirst-quenching; one might bear in mind that it is a non-alcoholic beer, and remember that brewers of real beer had launched an advertising slogan a good time back in German Switzerland which had passed into the language, insisting, like 'Guinness is good for you', on the nutritive value of beer—

'Bier ist mehr wert
Denn es hat Nährwert'—

and conclude from this that German Swiss did not need to be reminded. Against this one might point out that the French text draws attention to the similarity of 'Ex!' to beer in the belief that this is a recommendation to French speakers, who are less discriminating beer-drinkers than German speakers, while there is a tactful absence of reference of any kind to beer in the text intended for German and Italian speakers, presumably because German speakers find the idea of non-alcoholic beer repellent and Italian speakers hardly drink beer at all. And why are only the Italian speakers informed of the important fact that 'Ex!' keeps well, but are, like the French speakers, kept in the dark about the equally important fact that it should be drunk well chilled? However one sets about it, the distribution of information between the three languages makes no sense on the basis of group drinking habits, or even on the basis of group mores in general, for there is no reason to suppose for instance that German Swiss are more interested in their children's welfare than their French and Italian-speaking fellow-citizens. The assumption clearly is that a substantial section of the public understands more than one of the three languages, so that the advertising expert can use the different languages as means of variation.

1. G. G. Coulton, *Europe's Apprenticeship: a Survey of Medieval Latin with Examples,* London and Edinburgh 1940.
2. Birgit Stolt, *Die Sprachmischung in Luthers Tischreden* (= *Acta Universitatis Stockholmiensis, Stockholmer Germanistische Forschungen* 4), Stockholm 1964, esp. p. 17 ff. On group speech habits see p. 41.

3. Modernized text here after Leonard Forster, *Penguin Book of German Verse*, Harmondsworth 1957, p. 74. See also Johannes Bolte in *Festgabe an Karl Weinhold*, Leipzig 1896, and on this sort of poetry in the Romance area Paul Zumthor, 'Un problème d'ésthétique médiévale: l'utilisation poétique du bilinguisme', *Le Moyen Âge* LXVI (1960) p. 301 ff. In the seventh-century Irish poem *Sén Dé* (The Blessing of God) the author, after ten stanzas of Irish, based on the prayer in the breviary for the Commendation of the Soul, breaks out into Latin, which he alternates with the vernacular, and highlights it with the words: 'Regem regum rogamus In nostris sermonibus' (We beseech the King of Kings in [both] our languages). Latin, as the sacred language, is evidently felt to impart dignity and efficacy to the prayer at this point. See James Carney, ed., *Early Irish Poetry*, Cork 1965, p. 33. The fifteenth-century German poet Bruder Hans wrote a poem in praise of the Virgin in alternate lines of German, Latin, French and English. See Michael S. Batts, *Bruder Hansens Marienlieder*, Tübingen 1963 (= *Altdeutsche Textbibliothek* 58), p. 1 ff., and his *Studien zu Bruder Hansens Marienliedern*, Berlin 1964 (= *Quellen und Forschungen* 138), pp. 46 and 51.

4. Known to me from oral tradition in Basel. Not included in Albert Brenner, *Baslerische Kinder- und Volksreime*, Basel 1902. In Basel 'three' /drej/ does not rhyme with 'leg' /baj/; in dialects where 'leg' is /bej/ 'three' is /dry:/. The dialect is that of Baselland.

5. See in general A. R. Nykl, *Hispano-Arabic Poetry and its Relations with the Old Provençal Troubadours*, Baltimore 1946. S. M. Stern's first article appeared in *Al-Andalus* XIII (1948) p. 299 ff. Since then see S. M. Stern, *Les chansons mozarabes*, Palermo 1953 (reprinted Oxford 1964), esp. p. xvi; Klaus Heger, *Die bisher veröffentlichten Harǧas und ihre Deutungen* (= *Beihefte zur Zeitschrift für romanische Philologie* 101) Tübingen 1960, with extensive critical biliography to 1959; Peter Dronke, *Medieval Latin and the Rise of European Love-Lyric*, Oxford 1968, I, pp. 26 ff.; E. García Gómez, *Las jarchas romances*, Madrid 1965.

6. Joseph Linskill, *The Poems of the Troubadour Raimbaut de Vaqueiras*, The Hague 1964, p. 99.

7. A. Hoffmann von Fallersleben, *Niederländische Volkslieder* (= *Horae Belgicae* II), Hanover 1856, p. 242. It is odd that the lover should be characterized as a Norman, and yet understand Flemish, for Normandy and Flanders are separated by the whole of Picardy.

8. Helmuth von Glasenapp, *Die Literaturen Indiens von ihren Anfängen bis zur Gegenwart*, Wildpark-Potsdam 1929 (*Handbuch der Literaturwissenschaft*), p. 185; J. A. B. van Buitenen, *Two Plays of Ancient India: The Little Clay Cart and the Minister's Seal*, New York 1968, p. 9 ff.

9. For *Kameradschaft* see Siegfried Kracauer, *From Caligari to Hitler*, London 1949, p. 239 ff; for *La grande illusion* see Paul Rotha, *The Film till Now* with an additional section by Richard Griffith, London 1960, p. 532 ff; on *Friesennot* see Rotha and Griffith, op. cit., p. 589 and Joseph Wulf, *Theater und Film im Dritten Reich*, Gütersloh 1964, p. 339; the screenplay was based on a story by Werner Kortwich, *Friesennot*, Leipzig n.d. (= *Inselbücherei* no. 447, 1933).

10. Mr A. G. Parker kindly points out to me that these possibilities have been increasingly used, *e.g.* in Roberto Rossellini's *Paisà* (1946); Leopold Lindtberg's *Four in a Jeep* (1951), *Marie Louise* (1945) and *The Last Chance* (1946), all three made in Switzerland; and Sidney Gilliat's *State Secret* (1950), a British spy film in which the agents

of the foreign power speak a non-existent language called 'Vosnian' specially invented for this film (and apparently never used since).

11. The best early edition is *Theophili Folengi vulgo Merlini Coccaii Opus macaronicum notis illustratum*, 2 vols., Amsterdam 1768. Critical edition by A. Luzio, Bari 1927-28.

12. Brigitte Ristow, 'Maccaronische Dictung in Deutschland' in W. Kohlschmidt and Wolfgang Mohr edd., *Reallexikon der deutschen Literaturgeschichte*, Berlin 1965, II p. 259 ff., with bibliography. The standard works are still F. W. Genthe, *Geschichte der maccaronischen Poesie und Sammlung ihrer vorzüglichsten Denkmale*, Leipzig 1836, and J. A. Morgan, *Macaronic Poetry*, New York 1872.

13. A. D. Godley, *Reliquiae*, ed. C. R. L. Fletcher, Oxford 1926, I, p. 292; much anthologized since.

14. The examples in what follows are taken from H. J. Chaytor, *From Script to Print*, Cambridge 1945, chapter III, 'Language and Nationality'.

15. E. K. Chambers and F. Sidgwick, *Early English Lyrics*, London 1926, p. 15 ff.

16. K. K. Klein, ed., *Die Lieder Oswalds von Wolkenstein* (= *Altdeutsche Textbibliothek* 55) Tübingen 1962, p. 305. In one poem (p. 49) he claims to have acquired ten languages on his travels. A further virtuoso piece is Raimbaut de Vaqueiras' *descort* in six languages (Provençal, Italian, French, Gascon, Catalan and Galician-Portuguese), for which see Linskill, p. 191 ff.

17. Royall Tyler, *The Emperor Charles V*, London 1956, p. 20.

18. *Heptaméron* no. 24, quoted by Chaytor p. 25.

19. F. Grillparzer, *Sämtliche Werke*, ed. Albert Zipper, Leipzig (Reclam) n.d., VI, p. 195.

20. G. W. von Zedlitz, *The Search for a Country*, Wellington 1963, p. 163.

21. The term was coined by Weinreich, *Languages in Contact*, p. 99; see also Joshua A. Fishman, *Language Loyalty in the United States*, The Hague 1966.

22. Charles d'Orléans, *English Poems*, ed. R. Steele and M. Day (= *Early English Text Society Original Series* 215, 220) London 1941-46. Some scholars are inclined to doubt the attribution.

23. See e.g. F. Blatt, 'Sprachwandel im Latein des Mittelalters', *HV* XXVIII (1934) p. 22 ff., and A. Campbell, 'Some Linguistic Features of Early Anglo-Latin Verse', *Transactions of the Philological Society* 1953, p. 1 ff.

24. Mario Praz, *Studies in Seventeenth-Century Imagery*, Rome 1964; A. Henkel and A. Schöne, *Emblemata*, Stuttgart 1967; Holger Homann 'Prolegomena zu einer Geschichte der Emblematik', *Colloquia Germanica*, III (1968), p. 244.

25. Joshua Sylvester dedicated his translation to Du Bartas's *La Semaine* (*Bartas: his Deuine Weekes and Workes*, London 1605) to King James I with two sonnets, one in French and one in Italian.

3 Renaissance and Baroque

What is the purpose of these multilingual publications? In the first place doubtless a commercial one—the desire to reach a wider public and sell the book outside one's own frontiers, national or linguistic. A large part of this international public is itself polyglot. There will not have been many readers of Cats or Vaenius who only understood one of the languages represented in those works; most will have understood at least two. The variations which the polyglot texts offered provided an additional attraction. The seventeenth-century poet in all countries, and of course his readers too, had a different approach to poetry from the one which has become familiar to us since the Romantics. We are interested in personal expression of personal experience, something unique and individual which is peculiar to the poet, which constitutes his originality and his personal note, and which increases and deepens our knowledge of the potentialities of human nature. Until the Romantics poetry was concerned with the statement and presentation of socially acceptable themes; the poet was not talking for himself, in his own name, he was speaking to his society on behalf of that society; and because he had the gift of eloquent statement he was able to formulate familiar themes in a new, surprising and moving way. Powerful originality would have seemed idiosyncratic, unrepresentative and jarring, and would thus have defeated its own purpose.

The function of poetry then was statement and presentation. Contemporaries spoke of these two aspects in varying terms— 'utile et dulce', 'instruire et plaire'. The 'utile' was the statement of the socially acceptable, which was therefore instructive; the 'dulce' was the form in which the statement was presented, without which, however, instructive it might be, it would not please and therefore not achieve its aim. The techniques of statement and presentation were essentially the same irrespective of the language used. They had been inherited from antiquity and everybody learnt them at school in much the same form. It was therefore not difficult to use them in a foreign language as well as in one's own. Statement and formulation inevitably include re-statement and re-formulation, which give comparable pleasure to the poet and the reader. Thus mere re-statement in a different language provided an additional attraction, which the educated reader appreciated. And so the readers of the Dutch and Latin verses to Cats's emblems enjoyed them both, although in both the same thing was being said; what interested them was the different formulation of the same content in the two languages. It is common enough to find poets translating their own Latin verses; many German poets did this, and the subtitle 'Aus meinem Lateinischen', from my own Latin, is frequent in works of seventeenth-century poetry.

I have mentioned the way baroque poets liked to consider a theme from different or even contrary points of view, and I illustrated it by reference to the emblems of Cats. In the same way a given occasion may call forth not one, but three or four poems by the same poet. A common title in books of poetry is 'Aliud' or 'Ein Anderes', that is, another poem on the same theme. This is very clear in poems on particular public occasions. The German poet Georg Rudolf Weckherlin, about whom I shall have more to say later, wrote four poems on the death of Gustavus Adolphus of Sweden; one of them ran to over 100 lines, in which one would think that he had space to say everything he wanted, but that did not prevent him writing three others, one of them a sonnet, illuminating different aspects of the King's death.[1] Another German, J. L. Weidner, wrote seventeen (!) Latin epigrams on the death of Landgraf Moritz of Hessen in

1632, each of them considering the event from a different point of view.[2] A natural extension of this is to write the poems in different languages, and so we find Weidner's friend Julius Wilhelm Zincgref writing two German sonnets and two Latin epigrams on the same occasion. Seventy years earlier the Fleming Carolus Utenhove had produced a volume of poems in twelve languages on the death of King Henry II of France, most of them from his own hand.[3] Here the importance of simple re-formulation is very clear; all of the poems treat of a prayer deemed to be spoken by the King on his death-bed, and all consist of reformulations with variations, by Utenhove and his friends, of one basic text, written by Utenhove himself in Hebrew. These are public, dynastic, occasions, which call for display, but we shall see later that private occasions could be treated in the same way. Meanwhile it is worth considering the words of a much travelled Englishman with experience of foreign languages, Thomas Gawen of New College, Oxford, also on the occasion of the death of Landgraf Moritz of Hessen. He speaks of the re-markable linguistic knowledge of the departed, who was allegedly conversant even with Hungarian and English (both equally exotic languages for a West German prince in the first half of the seventeenth century), and goes on to say:

What Eloquence
And forceing Rhet'rick must arise from hence?
When ev'ry single thought might have the vse
Of soe vvell furnish'd Wardrobes, and mighd chuse
Figures that best befit itselve, to-day
Walke out in such a sute, to morrow may
It put on that, still vary'ing, as the sense
Should prompt, decorums, or the audience'.

The clothing image is significant; one clothes one's thoughts in different linguistic garments according to the requirements of 'decorum' on the one hand (that is, what the formal occasion demands) or of the audience on the other (that is, what language they understand). What Gawen here designates by clothes is what I earlier referred to as formulation, and he feels it to be an advantage if one can formulate in as many languages as possible, if one has an abundant linguistic equipment, or, to use his own term, 'well furnished wardrobes'. One can change one's language as one changes one's clothes, as circumstances may require.

Language is of course the medium in which all poets work, but this was true in a different sense for poets before Romanticism, for medieval, renaissance or baroque poets, than it has been since. Just as the artist need not always paint in oils, but also in water-colour, or may draw in pencil or charcoal or silverpoint, or may have recourse to woodcut or etching, so the poet may use more than one language. In this sense too Horace's adage 'ut pictura poesis' holds good. And just as the artist has to learn to handle these various media, so the poet too had to learn. One can think of very few German baroque poets (Grimmelshausen is one) who did not write their first verses in Latin—in an acquired language. Schooling was conducted mainly in Latin, and literature in the vernacular was not the concern of the school; on the other hand the writing of Latin and Greek verses was an elegant accomplishment, which the school did teach (and there are schools where it is still taught today). So it is that most poets proceed in their mother tongue as though they were writing Latin; it is but a short step from here to treating a modern foreign language in the same way.

The essential prerequisite for this is the availability of a ready-made means of expression, a stock of international formulae. In the renaissance and the seventeenth century these were very largely petrarchistic.[4] The foreign language must be a cultivated language, which, as Schiller put it, thinks and writes for you in the way to which you are accustomed. Schiller, writing from a modern standpoint, decries people who do this, and he was presumably referring not only to academic practitioners of Latin and Greek verse in his own day, but also to those who cautiously remain within the narrow bounds of an inherited poetic diction, when he wrote the distich:

Weil ein Vers dir gelingt in einer gebildeten Sprache,
Die für dich dichtet und denkt, glaubst du schon Dichter zu sein.

This reproach would not have been understood by most seventeenth-century poets. For them the cultivated language *par excellence* was Latin and, for the very learned, Greek, but according to circumstances French, Italian, Spanish and Dutch were also used. It is interesting to see how in the sixteenth century poets who write not merely competent but distinguished Latin poetry in difficult verse-forms often flounder in the vernacular for want of a model and a pre-established diction. For many renaissance poets it was actually easier to write in Latin than in their native language; the models were present to the mind, the

diction largely predetermined, and once one had reached a certain
level of competence Latin verses practically wrote themselves.
This is one of the reasons why poets translated their own Latin
verses, in order to help them to form their poetic diction in the
vernacular. This was one of the ways in which writers in different
countries introduced and acclimatized new fashions in literature
developed elsewhere, and made the European stock of styles and
themes available to their fellow countrymen.

One of these poets was Joachim du Bellay, whose three great
lyric cycles, *Antiquitez de Rome, Olive,* and *Les Regrets,* are
based to a large extent on his own Latin poetry. In this way he
helped to form the diction of the Pléiade; this French diction,
once formed, could be used by others in the same way as du
Bellay had used Latin. This is what the pioneer Dutch renaissance poet Jan van der Noot does.[5] Two of his works, *Lofsangh
van Brabandt* (1580) and *Cort Begrijp van de XII Boecken
Olympiados* (1579), appeared in bilingual editions, with French
and Dutch texts *en face.* If one compares the versions, it becomes
clear that the French texts present little of interest and that Van
der Noot as a French poet was a mediocre follower of Ronsard,
able to use the poetic diction forged by the Pléiade with reasonable skill and competence, but no more. If he had written
exclusively in French he would not merit any attention except
from very highly specialized investigators. But the parallel Dutch
texts are pioneer work, with which he introduced European
renaissance poetry into Dutch literature. More than that, they are
remarkably accomplished in technique, and by their music and
idealistic content they are still impressive and moving today.
Some of them are now standard anthology pieces, like Ronsard's
Quand vous serez bien vieille or Sidney's *My true love hath my
heart and I have his.* Van der Noot successfully transplants the
metre and the diction of the Pléiade into Dutch, thereby giving the
Low Countries their first considerable body of renaissance poetry
in the vernacular. It seems that he wrote the French versions
first; here he was operating with a 'cultivated language' in Schiller's
sense, which did half his work for him. On the basis of the French
versions he elaborated his new diction in Dutch by a laborious
process of what one might call 'auto-translation'. The result is
not polyglot poetry, but the work of a polyglot poet using his skill
to reformulate in one language what he had already formulated
in another. He too had the polyglot urge that we have already
seen in his elder contemporary Carolus Utenhove. He published

a number of editions of his collected poetic works (*Poeticsche Werken* 1580-91) in which each individual poem is accompanied by a prose commentary, in dialogue form, in which a learned man explains the poem for the benefit of a polyglot group of ladies who speak respectively Dutch, French, Italian, Spanish, Latin, Greek and German. Van der Noot was a native of Antwerp, which by virtue of its important trade connexions was one of the most polyglot cities in Europe; we may be sure that all these languages (except perhaps classical Greek) were actually spoken there. Even so, this commentary cannot be regarded as a functional literary reflexion of a polyglot community; it is simply an opportunity for Van der Noot to show off, though it is also an indication of his unusual awareness of the potentialities of different languages, which comes out in other ways too.

Van der Noot spent a great part of his life in exile; he fled from Antwerp in 1567 to escape the Duke of Alba and went first to London and later to Cologne. It was not enough for him that his works were written in both French and Dutch; he took care that some should also appear in English and German. His *Theatre oft Toon-neel* came out in London in 1568 in two separate editions, French and Dutch, and in the following year an English version was published which early attracted the attention of scholars. It was called *A Theatre for Voluptuous Worldlings*. All three versions consist of a prose treatise and a cycle of sonnets illustrated by engravings. The English translations of the poems are generally held to be the first published work of the young Edmund Spenser. The prose has been well described as 'a Calvinistic tract', but the poems with their accompanying engravings only need a motto to turn them into emblems, and indeed, they have often been considered as such by scholars. We are very close here to the sort of polyglot emblem book that I considered earlier, though in this case the different versions were published independently. On arrival in Cologne in 1573 he caused a German version to be produced. The translator is one Balthasar Froe, about whom very little is known. He was evidently a well-intentioned person, who did not fully understand what was required of him, but who did his best to reproduce the verse forms of the original. Van der Noot had used alexandrines and the ten syllable line known to the French as *vers commun*. There had been some experimentation with these forms in Dutch before Van der Noot, but none in German. The translator was therefore faced with a completely unfamiliar task, with which he grappled bravely but not always very successfully. Van der Noot's other great work, his *Olympia* epic, presents a similar picture. The epic was the most highly considered genre in the renaissance, and Van der Noot had planned a large scale work in twelve books (a hallowed number) depicting the journey of the human spirit through successive stages of temptation and purification until it reaches heaven, there to be joined in marriage with Olympia, the personification of heavenly love. In the event he was only able to produce an abridgement of it. The abridgement is extant in two different versions and three different languages. The first to be published was the German text, which appeared at Cologne in about 1576 under the title of *Das Buch Extasis*. Three years later, after his return to Antwerp, he produced a different version in parallel texts in French and Dutch presented *en face* with the double title *Cort Begrijp van de XII Boecken Olympiados* and *Abrégé de l'Olimpiade*. It is generally agreed that the German text represents a translation of an earlier version now lost to us, and it is thought that the translator is unknown; if he was Balthasar Froe he must have made very considerable progress in technique since the appearance of his earlier translation from Van der Noot. Here too he was faced with something which had no parallel in German, a book of positively aggressive modernity; he rose to the challenge and produced one of the most remarkable works of sixteenth-century German literature, in which he anticipated by nearly fifty years the important German stylistic and metrical reform carried out by Martin Opitz in 1624. The epic includes a number of lyrical passages, composed in sonnet form. These constituted a stiff test of the stylistic performance not only of the translator but also of Van der Noot himself as the 'auto-translator'. One of them is directly imitated from a poem of Ronsard's; we can see here particularly clearly the French model, the imitation of it in French, and the auto-translation into Dutch:[6]

> Ie suis vn demi-Dieu quand assis vis-à-vis
> De toy mon cher souci i'escoute les deuis,
> Deuis entre-rompus d'vn gracieux sou-rire,
> Souris qui me retient le cœur emprisonné:
> En contemplant tes yeux ie me pasme estonné,
> Et de mes pauures flancs vn seul vent ie ne tire.
>   Ma langue s'engourdist, vn petit feu me court
> Frétillant sous la peau; ie suis muet et sourd,
> Vn voile sommeillant dessus mes yeux demeure:
> Mon sang deuient glacé, le courage me faut,

Mon esprit s'euapore, et alors peu s'en faut
Que sans âme à tes pieds estendu ie ne meure.

Jan van der Noot: imitation of Ronsard (1579):

Ie suis vn demy Dieu, quant ie vois ma Maistresse,
Mon cœur, mon cher soucy: quant assis vis à vis
D'elle ie vois les yeux, escoutant les deuis:
Deuis, qu'on iugeroit deuis d'vne Deesse:
    Par fois entre-rompus, par gentille caresse,
Plus que mignardement d'vng gracieux soubris:
Vng souris, qui detient mon cœur fermement pris:
Car en voiant ses yeux ie me meurs de liesse.
    Ie voy dedans ses yeux Amour victorieux,
Qui va bas, qui va haut, tousiour me regardant:
Et son arc contre moy coup sur coup decochant.
    Ie reçoy plus de bien à regarder ses yeux,
Qu'à boire, ou qu'à manger, qu'à dormir, ni qu'à faire
Chose qui soit à l'âme ou au corps necessaire.

Jan van der Noot: auto-translation into Dutch (1579):

Dan ben ick een half Godt, wanneer ick ben geseten
By mijn Meestersse goed, en daer so med gemake
Heur goey maniren sie, en hoore heur sute wt-sprake,
Die dan ooc altemedt gebroken, en vergheten
    Wordt met een suet gelach, oft suchten quaet om weten.
In heur schoon ooghen suet daer ic altijdt na hake
Mercke ick de liefde reyn, die maect dat ick dus blake,
Die my euen-gedicht' deurwondt na sijn vermeten.
    Ken ben mijns sins gheen heer' wanneer ick heb' ghesoghen
Het bitter suet verghift wt heur sute bruyn ooghen
Dwelc my betoovert heeft, en houdt, euen-gedichte.
Ic ontfang meerder vreugt med heur oogen t'aenschouwen
Dan deur slaep', spijse, oft dranc, om d'lichaem
                                    t'onderhouwen.
So wel behaghen my heur deught en eerbaer wesen.

The character of each of these poems is completely different.
Ronsard's poem, which itself goes back to Catullus and beyond
that to Sappho, is a good poem by a good poet, not one of his
best, but the accomplished work of a master hand. Van der
Noot's French imitation is a mediocre work by a mediocre poet;
mediocre, not because it is an imitation—imitation was considered
a perfectly normal and respectable kind of poetic creation in the
sixteenth century and Ronsard himself did not consider it beneath

his dignity—but because wording, rhyme and versification are technically inferior. Ronsard's twelve lines have been expanded into
fourteen and his train of thought has been carried a little further by
skilful use of phrases from other poems by Ronsard—very much the
procedure employed by those who write Latin verses today, and
indeed Van der Noot is writing French as though he were writing
Latin, taking advantage of a pre-existing style and poetic diction
to elaborate on his model.

Many renaissance imitations are better poems than the works
they imitate, and it was theoretically possible for Van der Noot
to have improved on Ronsard. In his Dutch version he did in
fact improve on his own imitation. Here he has accomplished an
extremely difficult task; he has successfully adapted the subject
matter, style, diction and above all the metre of the French to
the completely different requirements of the Dutch language, so
it is not surprising to find him occasionally resorting to padding
to get his rhyme. It is not a direct translation, for in his second
quatrain he departs from the French, takes up the motif of love
which wounds his heart from the first tercet of the French, and
in his first Dutch tercet he departs altogether from the image of
love walking up and down in the beloved's eyes and uses a
rather more well-worn petrarchistic commonplace about the trans-
porting effect the lady's eyes have on him, but he returns in the
last tercet to a reformulation of his own French. It is thus more
than just a translation.

Van der Noot aimed at reproducing the metre and the rhythm
of French verse in Dutch; 'sometimes he seems to have turned
over the French lines in his mind until replicas of astonishing
rhythmical closeness flowed from his pen, lines in which the
very lilt of the original is reproduced without appreciable loss
of freshness . . . Truly a technical feat and one of a kind through
which Van der Noot did in fact acquire the French rhythm so
thoroughly that he was soon able to achieve it independently'.[7]
(This process in itself is less unusual than it might seem. I have
a respected colleague in another subject who emigrated from
Germany in 1935 and has since published mainly in English.
He tells me that, for many years now, if he needs to write in
German, he drafts his text in English first and then translates
it into German.)

Here, in the early days of renaissance and baroque literature in
Northern Europe, stands Jan van der Noot, who by his personal
achievement and by his inspiring example gave an important

stimulus to the development of a more modern poetry in Dutch, English and German. I can think of no poet of his times who exploited as thoroughly and as successfully as he did the possibilities of auto-translation and none who worked with such consistency and virtuosity in two vernaculars at the same time. In the case of Van der Noot we have a poet who, though French was probably an acquired language for him, may fairly be called bilingual in more than the technical sense. Moreover he was writing for a bilingual province, Brabant, and thus wrote his poetry in two languages. In the dedication of one of his works to the States of Brabant he emphasizes the point that he had 'in de twee talen die in Brabant natuerliick ghesproken worden, ghedicht ende ghesongen' (written and sung in the two languages naturally spoken in Brabant).[8] This circumstance justifies his bilingual poetry as the functional reflexion of an actual social situation. But there are other polyglot poets in this period for whom this justification does not hold.

There are of course always cases in which a definite external occasion prompts the use of a particular language. And so the German Neolatin poet Vincentius Fabricius, on a sea journey between Amsterdam and Hamburg in 1634, wrote a series of gracious and accomplished *vers de société* in Dutch to two Amsterdam ladies.[9] In the same way the court poet of the Duke of Württemberg, Georg Rudolf Weckherlin, welcomed the King of England's ambassador, the Scot James Hay, with a panegyric in English verse in 1619.[10] With Weckherlin we enter a domain where the use of several languages is evidently normal. At the Court of Stuttgart Weckherlin produced poetry in German, French and English, and it is known that he also wrote poetry in Latin. The parallel use of his native German and of other languages in poetry is one of the traits which go to make up his individuality as a poet. But we must ask the question: what is the social justification for it? That is, for whom did he write his foreign language works?

It is clear that they were written for the Württemberg Court. His first publications are descriptions of court festivities, which one might compare with the full programme notes sold at productions of 'Son et Lumière', describing the show and giving the text of the songs and the speeches. These were in German, but occasionally the presence of exalted guests from outside caused programme notes in other languages too to be provided. In 1616, on the occasion of a dynastic christening, they were in German

and English, for the guest of honour was the consort of the
Elector Palatine, Elizabeth, daughter of James I of England. In
his introduction to the English version Weckherlin is at some
pains to point out that he produced it at the express command
of his Prince.[11] The following texts, German and English versions
of the same poem, may serve as an example of what he could do:

Die spiegelmacher an das Frawenzimmer

Nymfen, deren anblick mit wunderbarem schein
Kan unser hertz zugleich hailen oder versehren;
Und deren angesicht, ein spiegel aller ehren,
Uns erfüllet mit forcht, mit hofnung, lust und pein:
Wir bringen unsern kram von spiegeln klar und rein,
Mit bit, ihr wollet euch zuspieglen nicht beschweren:
Die spiegel, welche uns ewere schönheit lehren,
Lehren euch auch zumahl barmhertziger zu sein.
   So gelieb es euch nun, mit lieblichen anblicken
Erleuchtend gnädiglich unsern leuchtenden dantz,
Und spieglend euch in uns, uns spiegler zu erquicken:
Wann aber ungefehr ewerer augen glantz
Uns gar entfreyhen solt, so wollet uns zugeben,
Das wir in ewerm dienst fürhin stehts mögen leben.

The Looking-Glass-Makers to the Ladies

Unto you daintie Nymph's, that by the dazling light
Of your sweet shining eyes doe all treasur's display:
That by wonderful look's of a celestiall might
Can gods and men at once both rejoyce and dismay:
   Unto you, by whose beam's this night is like the day,
Wee doe offer our ware, that shews you your faire sight,
Ev'n as your brighter eyes, true mirrors of delight,
Doe teach us vertues all but with one gentle ray.
   Therefore Ladies most fair (we pray) doe not disdaine
T'adorne our ware and us, with your heavenly glaunce,
Glaunce, that could the whole world without the sunne
                                                    maintaine,
   But if your look's should spoile our libertie perchaunce,
Then, kind, doe graunt thus much, that after this our dance,
We may all with our shop at your service remaine.

Two years later there was a masque to celebrate the arrival of
Duke Julius Friedrich of Württemberg with his newly wedded
bride Anna Sabina, Duchess of Holstein, and this time too there
were bilingual texts, distributed by the masquers, in German and

French. They are prefaced by a sonnet by Weckherlin addressed
to the Duke and his princely brothers; it is written in French.
There was no special reason for the use of this particular language
on this occasion; there were no eminent French guests, and the
bridal pair were both Germans; moreover, it is clear from documents in the Stuttgart archives that the Duke and his brothers
were anything but proficient in the French language. The use of
French for these texts is not functionally justified. No explanation
is given; it was apparently taken as a matter of course, a matter,
in fact, of 'decorum' in Thomas Gawen's sense. The foreign
language imparted an additional brilliance to the festivities, and
the audience doubtless appreciated the varying formulations in
the two languages, much as the readers of Cats's emblems will
have done. The two works appeared in the same year.

As with the emblems, this state of affairs presupposes a public
able to appreciate a literary work from more than one linguistic
aspect. In this there is no difference between bourgeois Dutch
Zealand and courtly Stuttgart, so that we may expect similar conditions elsewhere. Polyglot though this public was, and interested
in linguistic differences, it was not, as many have thought, hostile
to its own vernacular. Weckherlin himself was a pioneer of courtly
renaissance poetry in German, and on a similar occasion writes
verses in which he defends the German language against inter-
ference from outside:[12]

> Nein, es ist nicht mehr noht, mit Welsch-vermischter Sprach
> Der Ausländer Wollust und Freuden zu erzehlen:
> Teutschland empfacht dadurch weder Gespöt noch Schmach,
> Sondern hat in sich selbs noch Frewd gnug zuerwöhlen.

No, there is no longer any need to rehearse the joys and plea-
sures of foreigners in Frenchified language. Germany will
[henceforth] incur neither mockery nor shame in this way, but
[on the contrary] has sufficient pleasurable resources of her own.

Tournaments and masques are a patriotic act, to which the German language is entirely appropriate. Even in his introduction to
the English version of one of these works he points out that though
this version was made at the command of the prince, 'I shall
indevor *the more* to honour *in German* the gallant English nation'.
Literary activity in the foreign language is not pursued at the
expense of that in the mother tongue but parallel with it, and
indeed the two are thought of as complementary. In 1636, long
after the reform of German poetry by Opitz in 1624, a North

German poet, Zacharias Lund, makes exactly this point.[13] Philip
von Zesen, one of the most prominent defenders of German
poetry in the seventeenth century, published over twenty poems
in Dutch and several in French. There were good external reasons
for this, for Zesen lived in Holland and maintained friendly relations with a circle of cultivated ladies of title in Utrecht and
Amsterdam, for whom he composed a number of poems in
German and in Dutch. But he also wrote an Ode to Sylvia, extant
in Dutch and French but not in German.[14] Here too we must
presuppose a society in which the poem could be appreciated in
both versions, a society in which poetry circulated in various
languages. It was probably for the Utrecht ladies that Zesen
wrote the little Latin epigram which had the honour of being
translated into Dutch by the greatest of Dutch poets, his contemporary Joost van den Vondel. In Utrecht moreover lived the
famous polyglot bluestocking Anna Maria van Schurman, the
wonder of the learned world. Either she or her niece Anna
Margarethe wrote the verses for Zesen which adorn the engraved
portrait which appears as the frontispiece to his works:

> Le Soleil des Almans, leur Varro, leur Homère
> L'illustre Zesen cy deguise sa lumière
> Sous l'ombre de ces traits. Mais veux tu voir l'esclat
> De son esprit divin, voyez son *Assenat.*

In these lines we have the praise of a German poet, and of his
German novel *Assenat,* formulated by a Dutchwoman in French.
She could just as well have written it in Dutch or in Latin or in
German; Zesen would have understood her just as well. The
reasons why she chose to do it in French are hidden from us.
The actual content of the lines is a well-worn commonplace, which
could slip easily into any language. One thing is clear: in circles
such as these language is material, with which one operates, with
which one forms or formulates something. The choice between
one language and another is much less important.

There were circles of this kind in other Dutch towns as well.
In them was rooted the literary life of the Dutch Golden Age,
and in few of them was Dutch the only language current. In
academic Leiden and in certain circles elsewhere Latin was a
close competitor; elsewhere French, Italian, sometimes even English, were cultivated alongside Dutch. In Amsterdam even the
young Gerbrand Adriaensz Bredero, who of all the major literary
figures of the Dutch Golden Age was closest to the people and its

poetry, felt obliged to write at least one sonnet in what he himself calls his 'bad school French'.[15] But it is important to notice that here, as in Germany, it was precisely in these circles that literature in the mother tongue was most intensively cultivated and most intelligently criticized. A characteristic example is the circle which P. C. Hooft, the greatest Dutch poet of his age next to Vondel, brought together at his castle of Muiden outside Amsterdam. Hooft's own work deserves our attention for a moment.

We have seen in the case of Van der Noot how a writer can form his style in an as yet largely untried vernacular by a process of auto-translation. This is an early stage. Thirty years later, when the work of Van der Noot and his generation had had its effect, we can look into the workshop of a considerable poet who was at the height of his powers, who was in complete stylistic control of his mother tongue and who was about to enrich its literature with his published work. In January 1605 Brechje Spiegels, the woman who had inspired Hooft's finest poetry, died suddenly, only a few days after he had written her a justly famous love lyric. Hooft dated all his poems, and the dates here are important. Brechje Spiegels died on January 15.[16] Etiquette would normally require a poet closely associated with the family to produce a dirge of some kind almost as soon as the news reached him. Hooft, shattered, remained silent for four days. On January 19 he wrote an epitaph in Dutch consisting of fourteen short lines, in which he tries to express and control his grief, as the compli-cated and tortured syntax shows. It is as though he was trying to pack everything into these few lines, and he seems to have realized that the attempt had not succeeded. On January 22 he tried to express himself more simply and turned to another language; he wrote one Latin distich and six lines of French verse, moving but rather clumsy, and not less touching because they are clumsy:

> Brechie Spiegels, las!
> Ci gît, gentille éteinte.
> Au monde, à son trépas,
> Dirent adieu en plainte
> Bonté discrète et sainte,
> Sage gayeté de mœurs,
> Sincerité non feinte,
> Charmeresse des cœurs.

The formulation is abstract: the personified virtues depart with the departed. The only concrete thing in the poem is the departed herself, who is mentioned by name. But compared with his first attempt in Dutch he has achieved a remarkable degree of simplification. On the following day, January 23, he was evidently not satisfied with this simplicity and attempted an epitaph in four compressed Latin distichs; on the same day he wrote another of five lines in Italian, which he immediately translated into Dutch. Within the week he had therefore made six separate attempts in four different languages, none of which seem to have satisfied him. This is in itself a measure of the emotional stress he was under. But he had not only tried out different possibilities, he had also achieved a certain distance from his subject; for some time he wrote nothing more on it. Not until much later, it seems, was he able to distil what he had already written into six wonderfully concentrated lines in Dutch. They contained no word of his own personal grief, which is conveyed subtly but poignantly through the movement and the melody of the verse alone. What was abstract in the earlier versions has been transposed into the concrete and everything turns on the dead beloved. Her name is no longer mentioned, but what need? She is there before us:

> Groot van geest en klein van leden,
> Groen van jaren, grijs van zeden,
> Lieflijk zonder lafferij,
> Goeilijk zonder hovaardij,
> Rein van hart inzonderheid
> Was zij, die hier onder leit.

Here is a very rough literal rendering:

> Stout of spirit and slender of stature, green in years but grey in manners, charming without sentimentality, kind without arrogance, pure in heart above all else was she who lies below [this stone].

But there are nuances impossible to reproduce in a translation. The words I have rendered as 'spirit', 'manners', 'charming', could also mean 'intellect', 'moral virtues' and 'warm-hearted' or 'inspiring love', and we may be certain that the poet intended these meanings to be simultaneously present. The Roman author whom Hooft admired most was Tacitus, and his influence may be felt in the poet's attempts at compression in some of the earlier versions of this poem. Here he has not tried to compress but to select, and to concentrate by utilizing the resources of ambiguity which the Dutch language afforded him. Here too, poetry in foreign languages stands in the service of poetry in the mother-tongue, but in a quite different way from Van der Noot's. We can watch the poet working his way up laboriously from language to language until he finally achieves his best—in his mother-tongue.

Hooft brought a distinguished company together at the meetings in his castle. The poets Constantijn Huygens, Joost van den Vondel and Maria Tesselschade Visscher; the architect of the Amsterdam City Hall, Jacob van Campen; the singer Francisca Duarte; the great Latinist Caspar Barlaeus; and many others. An important factor was the presence of educated, intelligent and talented women. Works circulated among them in manuscript which were read aloud, discussed, and criticized. Barlaeus wrote almost exclusively in Latin; Hooft mainly in Dutch, but also, as we have seen, in Latin, French and Italian. Huygens wrote not only in Dutch but also in Latin, French and Italian and occasionally in Spanish, Greek, English and German. This polyglot fashion did not prevent the closest attention being paid to the practice of literature in the mother-tongue, to questions of style and diction in Dutch, and some of the works which circulated in this group are now among the classics of Dutch literature. It was precisely the general knowledge of other literatures which enabled Hooft and his friends to apply high critical and intellectual standards, and it was their practical acquaintance with problems of literary craftsmanship in other languages which sharpened their sense of what could be achieved in Dutch. The corresponding phenomenon in France was the Hôtel de Rambouillet, where Voiture did not disdain to write Spanish verses or Ménage Italian.[17] That the tradition persisted in France is shown by the ease with which Molière handles Italian when he had a mind to, an ease which he can assume in his audience too.[18] The most many-sided figure of this circle was Constantijn Huygens, the father of the great mathematician Christiaan Huygens. He was not only a polyglot poet but an active composer. The arts however were only something for his leisure hours, as the title of his collected Latin poems hinted—Otia. His time was mainly occupied by his arduous duties as secretary to Prince Frederick Henry of Nassau and the various diplomatic missions these involved. With him we enter the world of international diplomacy, in which Georg Rudolf Weckherlin was also at home. A career diplomat in our own day is expected to have some skill in foreign languages, but hardly to the extent of writing poetry in them. The French verses of Huygens would fill a substantial volume, and so

would his Latin poems, apart from his voluminous production
in Dutch. Much of his work consists in witty formulation of
proverbial wisdom or neat expression of an ingenious thought—a
favourite use for poetry in the seventeenth century. This sort of
wit can be exercised in any language. Huygens loves to take an
amusing remark or a pithy saying and reformulate it in verse in
three or four different languages with up to six different versions.
These were five-finger exercises, but sometimes, when he applies
this procedure to more serious subjects, the foreign language
version succeeds better than the Dutch. His poems circulated
among his friends, and from the names of the persons to whom
he addressed them one could go far towards reconstructing the
composition of this whole cultivated class in Holland for which
he and so many others—foreigners like Philip von Zesen amongst
them—wrote. It would be an interesting exercise in the sociology
of Western European literature in the seventeenth century, for
Huygens had contacts not only all over the Netherlands, but also
in England, France and Germany. This multilingual literature
is admittedly something cultivated in small groups, and much of
it could be described in John Betjeman's words as 'Dear private
giggles of a private world';[19] but these groups were in personal
or epistolary contact with one another all over Europe; the circles
intersect and overlap. Huygens himself was a sort of intersection
point. In one of his Latin poems[20] he expressed the attitude under-
lying much of this polyglot verse-writing. Caspar Barlaeus had
written a Latin poem in 1625 in which he adjured his friends—
of whom Huygens was one—to give up writing poetry in the
vernacular and to devote themselves entirely to the Roman and
the Attic muses. When reading Huygens's reply one expects a
sort of anticipation of the 'querelle des anciens et des modernes',
but he takes quite another line. After mentioning his own efforts
in the different vernaculars he goes on to say: ' I have come to
realize that the poet is not born or nourished from one Castalian
spring alone. He is at home in any country, he is a citizen of the
world'—'Omne solum vati patria est, ille incola mundi'—and he
is the same to all men—'ille omnibus idem'. The language in
which he writes is evidently of secondary importance only.

   Among those who were in correspondence with Huygens was
the German Georg Rudolf Weckherlin. I have already mentioned
his occasional poetry in English and French written for the
Württemberg Court. In 1619 he settled in England, and from this
time onwards he published German poetry only, though we know

that he continued to write in other languages too. We have in manuscript a cycle of poems in four languages—German, French, English and Latin—on the death of the daughter of his patron, William Trumbull, English resident in Brussels. Only the German poem was published.[21] Weckherlin's main concern as a poet was with poetry in German; despite his proficiency in the other languages they were less important to him, and so the French, English and Latin poems in this cycle—and for all we know in others as well—were never printed. Their importance was restricted to this one occasion, and their function was ornamental—analogous to that of the framework of symbolic ornament with which he himself decorated the manuscript, in order to make each page of it look like a contemporary memorial tablet on a church wall. For the recipient they were doubtless also ornamental, but in a different way. There is nothing in what we know of Trumbull (and we know a good deal)[22] to suggest that he knew any German. For him the message was contained in the English, French and Latin poems which he could read—the German was purely decorative. But both poet and patron knew and appreciated the value of ornament. Here, as with the emblem books, nothing is said in any language which could not have been said in any other.

Weckherlin did however write one poem in English during his years in England which could not have been written in German. He had recently been appointed secretary to the Secretary of State, an important official post in which his knowledge of languages was useful. It involved constant attendance at Court, and the Court moved with the King on his progresses from place to place —from Whitehall to Newmarket to Oatlands to Hampton Court and so on—so that he was often absent from home for long stretches at a time. His wife, who was English, seems to have asked him what he actually did while he was away. In answer he wrote her from Newmarket a charming verse epistle of about 100 lines in English, sketching his day from the moment he got up, and looking forward at the end to a reunion with his wife and family.[23]

> [. . .] Now when I am quite ready, and haue layd
> All my things vp in order You know how;
> I thinking then on thee, my boy, my maid,
> And of all those, that doe concerne me now,
> I doe appeare (though hopefull, yet afraid)
> And cast myself before My God full low.

To him I sing due praise with mouth and hart,
Of him for things amisse I mercie craue,
I craue his ayd and grace for Vs apart,
I craue his grace our frends and foes to saue,
In generall I pray him not to part
From his poore flock for which his Sonne he gaue.
I doe not mean to boast here of deuotion;
He that doth brag of holinesse of life
Hath of the Sp'rit of pride, of pride, the motion,
And proues betweene his wordes and workes great strife;
To seem, but not to be, good is his notion.
I write to me when I write to my Wife. [. . .]

The style is an easy *parlando*—the unaffected utterance of a husband talking to his wife—and it does not exclude the occasional
little joke. This could not have been written in German because
at the time it was written—1627, a mere three years after Martin
Opitz's reform of German poetry—German literature had not
yet developed an informal conversational style, and indeed did
not do so for over a hundred years. German poets were concen-
trating on a lofty style suitable for important occasions. Moreover,
the social class which in England favoured a conversational style,
an educated, prosperous and assured middle class, was absent
in Germany in the seventeenth century and did not begin to make
its presence felt in German literature until the advent of Gottsched
in 1725. Weckherlin's epistle in English verse is thus an organic
product, of quite a different kind from the other seventeenth-
century poems in foreign languages which we have considered,
and as the work of a German poet it anticipates future developments in German literature. As a piece of English writing it is
more than just competent; it is quite accomplished, and stands in
a distinguishable English tradition; moreover, it is much more
up to date as English verse than anything we know of that he
had written in English before. Yet he himself evidently regarded
it as a private trifle, not deserving publication.

Weckherlin remained in the service of England until he retired
in 1649 as Latin Secretary under the Commonwealth. His successor
in that office was another poet, but an incomparably greater one
—John Milton. He too was a polyglot poet, who wrote in Latin,
Greek and Italian besides English. His attitude to his poems in
foreign languages was quite different from Weckherlin's; precisely
because English literature was more securely based than German
literature, he saw no reason to suppress them, and included them

as a matter of course among his English verses. Of his published *Sonnets* no. 1 is in English, nos. 2 - 6 are in Italian, nos. 7 - 10 in English. The Italian poems are in fact not all sonnets; one is a canzone. However natural it evidently seemed to him to write poetry in foreign languages, it was none the less a problem which occupied his mind, and he is one of the few polyglot poets of his age who has anything to say about it. His early sonnets, whether in English or Italian, have an intimate character; they arise from private occasions and are mostly addressed to friends; again, as in Holland and in France, the socially conditioned poetry of a small group. The Italian poems are among his earliest and date from before 1638, before the young poet had ever set foot in Italy. Apart from his seventh Latin elegy they are the only love poems of his that we have, and their editor has well observed that 'among Milton's early poems those in which he speaks of his own feelings with least reserve are those in which his self-revelation is veiled by the use of a foreign language'.[24] It is a different case from Weckherlin's English epistle. It would be foolish to suppose that Milton even as a young man had not got the technical means at his disposal to say in English what he says in Italian—or in Latin. It must therefore be that he preferred not to, or could not for some inner personal reason. The Italian poems are addressed, with one exception, to a young lady named Emilia, who came of an Italian family long settled in London. There is no reason to think that she would not have understood him had he written in English. In the one exceptional sonnet, addressed not to Emilia but to his friend Diodati, he describes her as follows:

    Diodati—e te'l dirò con meraviglia—
Quel ritroso io, ch'Amor spreggiar solea,
E de' suoi lacci spesso mi ridea,
Già caddi, ov'uom dabben talor s'impiglia.
    Nè treccie d'oro nè guancia vermiglia
M'abbaglian sì, ma sotto nuova idea
Pellegrina bellezza che'l cuor bea,
Portamenti alti onesti, e nelle ciglia
    Quel sereno fulgor d'amabil nero,
Parole adorne di lingua più d'una,
E'l cantar che di mezzo l'emispero
    Traviar ben può la faticosa Luna;
E degli occhi suoi avventa sì gran fuoco
Che'l incerar gli orecchi mi fia poco.

Diodati—and I shall tell it thee with wonder—my stubborn self, that was wont to despise Love and often laughed at his snares, has now fallen where sometimes an upright man is entangled. Neither tresses of gold nor rosy cheek beguiles me thus; but, under a new form, strange beauty charms my heart, manners that are lofty and modest, and in her gaze a calm radiance of gentle black, delightful speech in languages more than one, and singing that from the mid hemisphere might lure the labouring moon; and from her eyes there darts such fire that to close my ears would avail me but little.

The description owes much to the stereotype of the Petrarchan lady—even to the black eyelashes and the accomplished singing—but it may well have been true for all that, for this was an ideal which young ladies all over Europe tried to live up to. But it contains one non-Petrarchan trait: 'Parole adorne di lingua più d'una'—elegant speech in more than one language. The whole picture he gives, and not least this particular trait, agrees with the impression we have of cultivated women in France and in the Low Countries—Madame de Rambouillet, Julie d'Angennes, or the ladies of Hooft's circle. He writes for Emilia and he writes in Italian because she wishes it. His age-mates, he says in his canzone, make fun of him and the 'additional burden' which he is laying on himself thereby:

> Ridonsi donne e giovani amorsi,
> M'accostandosi attorno, e 'Perchè scrivi,
> Perchè tu scrivi in lingua ignota e strana,
> Verseggiando d'amor, e come t'osi?
> Dinne, se la tua speme sia mai vana,
> E de' pensieri la miglior t'arrivi.'
> Così mi van burlando, 'Altri rivi,
> Altri lidi t'aspettan ed altre onde,
> Nelle cui verdi sponde
> Spuntati ad or a la tua chioma
> L'immortal guiderdon d'eterne frondi.
> Perchè alle spalle tue soverchia soma?'
>   Canzon, dirotti, e tu per me rispondi.
> Dice mia donna, e 'l suo dir è il mio cuore,
> 'Questa è lingua di cui si vanta Amore'.

Amorous youths and maidens gather about me with mirth, and 'Why dost thou write?' they ask, 'Why dost thou write in a strange and unknown tongue, making verses of love, and how dost thou dare? Tell us; that so thy hope may not be vain, and the best of thy wishes be fulfilled.' And thus they jest with me

—'Other streams, other banks await thee, and other waves, on whose green margin there sometimes grows, to crown thy head, the immortal guerdon of unfading leaves. Why place upon thy shoulders a superfluous load?' Song, I will tell thee, and thou shalt answer for me. My lady says, and her words are my heart: 'This is the language in which Love takes pride'.

The reason is that his lady has said: 'Questa è lingua di cui si vanta Amore'; in other words, Italian is the language of love, the appropriate language for love poetry. Milton here, doubtless for inner reasons of his own, is taking up the medieval convention whereby the choice of language was determined by the literary genre. It is worth noticing that he wrote no love poetry in English. The Emperor Charles V had thought that Italian was the language to use with women; this was in the sixteenth century. But even forty years after Milton's poem the convention was still alive enough for Molière to think it worth while to make fun of it. In the first interlude to *Le Malade imaginaire* he shows us Polichinelle preparing to serenade his hard-hearted beloved: 'Je viens voir si je ne pourrai point adoucir ma tigresse par une sérénade. [. . .] O nuit! ô chère nuit! porte mes plaintes amoureuses jusque dans le lit de mon inflexible.' He then sings some stanzas in rather indifferent Italian:

> Notte e dì v'amo e v'adoro,
> Cerco un sì per mio ristoro;
> Ma se voi dite di no,
> Bell' ingrata, io morirò,

and gets beaten up for his pains.

For Milton, as for Huygens, and the men of their time, there is no mystique about languages; they are simply different media in which a poet can work—and can be expected to work.

Most of the works I have dealt with so far can be considered, from one point of view at least, as five-finger exercises. From the sociological angle they can be seen as belonging to Western European 'poésie précieuse' in the wider sense. This has been defined[25] as a literature which arises in small groups of cultivated people and which aims at producing an elegant intellectual and aesthetic pleasure, without however endangering the civilized atmosphere essential to the group. Poets therefore avoid anything disquieting, and within the framework of existing social convention they tend to treat innocuous themes in what has been aptly called a kind of 'lyric Esperanto'—whatever language they happen to be writing in. In circumstances such as these, five-finger exercises can be socially justified if they are performed with sufficient elegance. But the case of Milton does not stand alone; it sometimes happens that the poet can express his feelings more freely in the foreign language than in his own. It is as if the use of the foreign language removes certain inhibitions; the formal exercise suddenly acquires 'soul'.

Hugo von Hofmannsthal quotes with particular approval a tiny story by Peter Altenberg[26] about the half-conscious sentimental relationship between a small girl and a very grown-up young man. He is listening to her doing her piano practice. Suddenly he is unexpectedly moved by a recurring series of splendid phrases. He asks what she is playing and she replies 'Bertini No. 18; every time I play that I think of you', without being able to explain any further. Greatly touched, he walks quietly up and down and she goes on practising—Bertini no. 19, Bertini no. 20, 21, 22, 23, but the soul of it was gone.

'Aber die Seele kam nicht wieder'—even if there is no 'soul', exercises of this kind are a necessary preliminary to high quality performance. If you have not worked through the exercises of Bertini and Czerny you will not be able to play Beethoven's sonatas. And Hofmannsthal elsewhere spoke of languages as musical instruments.

1. G. R. Weckherlin, *Gedichte*, ed. H. Fischer, 3 vols. (= *Bibliothek des Literarischen Vereins Stuttgart* 199-200, 245) Tübingen 1898 ff. nos. 147-149. On Weckherlin in general see Leonard Forster, *G. R. Weckherlin; zur Kenntnis seines Lebens in England*, Basel 1944.
2. The poems mentioned written on this occasion are all printed in the memorial publication *Mausoleum Mauritianum*, Kassel 1635-40, three volumes.
3. *Epitaphium in mortem Herrici Gallorum Regis Christianissimi eius nominis secundi per C. Utenhovium* [. . .] *et alios duodecim linguis*, Paris 1560. On Utenhove, see W. Janssens, *Charles Utenhove*, Diss Nijmegen 1939 and J. A. van Dorsten, *The Radical Arts*, Leiden 1970.
4. Leonard Forster, 'European Petrarchism as Training in Poetic Diction', *Italian Studies* XVIII (1963) p. 19 ff, reprinted and amended in *The Icy Fire, Five Studies in European Petrarchism*, Cambridge 1969.
5. Leonard Forster, 'Jan van der Noot und die deutsche Renaissancelyrik' in Reinhold Grimm and Conrad Wiedemann, edd., *Literatur und Geistesgeschichte, Festgabe für Heinz Otto Burger*, Berlin 1968, p. 70 ff, with bibliography.
6. C. A. Zaalberg, *The Olympia Epics of Jan van der Noot*, Assen 1956, pp. 269, 184.

7. Theodoor Weevers, *Poetry of the Netherlands in its European Context*, London 1960, p. 69.
8. Jan van der Noot, *Lofsang van Braband: Hymne de Braband*, ed. C. A. Zaalberg, Zwolle 1958, p. 61.
9. Printed in Zacharias Lund, *Allerhand artige deutsche Gedichte*, Hamburg 1636, p. 132 ff.
10. Weckherlin, *Gedichte*, III, p. 3 ff.
11. Weckherlin, *Gedichte*, I, pp. 8, 9, 41. The wedding masque for the Duke, ibid. p. 79 ff.
12. Ibid., p. 78.
13. Zacharias Lund, *Allerhand artige deutsche Gedichte*, fo. B4 recto.
14. Mostly in Zesen's *Dichterisches Rosen- und Liljentahl*, Hamburg 1670; see also Weevers, op. cit., p. 92. On the social circle interesting details in W. Graadt van Roggen, *Een Stichtsche sleutelroman uit de zeventiende eeuw*, Utrecht n.d.
15. G. A. Bredero, *Dramatische Werken*, ed. J. A. N. Knuttel, II, Amsterdam 1924, p. 102; for the poem see his *Liederen, Gedichten, Proza*, ed. J. A. N. Knuttel, Amsterdam 1929, p. 298.
16. The poems in all languages on the death of Brechje Spiegels are to be found in P. C. Hooft, *Gedichten*, ed. F. A. Stoett and P. Leendertz, Amsterdam 1899, I, p. 41 ff. I have modernized the spelling in the quotations. On Hooft in general see H. W. van Tricht, *P. C. Hooft*, Haarlem 1951, and Sir Herbert Grierson's lecture 'Two Dutch Poets', reprinted in his *Essays and Addresses*, London 1940. Since these lectures were given the poems have been the subject of an interesting rhetorical analysis, which however takes little account of the polyglot aspect, by S. F. Witstein, *Funeraire poëzie in de Nederlandse Renaissance* (= *Neerlandica Traiectina* XXVII), Assen 1969, p. 190 ff.
17. *Œuvres de M. de Voiture*, Paris 1713, II, p. 74; *Ægidii Menagii Poëmata, octava editio*, Amsterdam 1687, contains verses in French, Latin, Greek, and Italian; on pp. 327 and 338 Italian verses addressed to Mme de Rambouillet herself.
18. Italian companies played at the Hôtel de Bourgogne in Molière's day and before; see L. Moland, *Molière et la comédie italienne*, Paris 1867, and H. Carrington Lancaster, *History of French Dramatic Literature in the Seventeenth Century*, Baltimore 1929 ff, Part IV, vol. ii, p. 599 ff.
19. John Betjeman, *Summoned by Bells*, London 1960, p. 98. On the Muiden Circle see John F. Flinn. 'La préciosité dans la littérature néerlandaise: l'œuvre de Maria Tesselschade', *Revue de littérature comparée* XL (1966), p. 65 ff, with bibliography.
20. Constantijn Huygens, *Gedichten*, ed. J. A. Worp, Arnhem 1892-99, II, p. 122. There is as yet no satisfactory monograph on this versatile figure, but see Rosalie L. Colie, *Some Thankfulnesse to Constantine*, The Hague 1956, and A. G. H. Bachrach, *Sir Constantine Huygens and Britain*, Leiden 1962, vol. I, the second volume of which is eagerly awaited.
21. Leonard Forster, 'Ein viersprachiger Gedichtzyklus G. R. Weckherlins', *Jahrbuch der Schiller-Gesellschaft* I (1957), p. 11 ff.
22. His extensive correspondence is calendared in the Historical Manuscripts Commission's *Report on the Manuscripts of the Marquess of Downshire*, vols. II-IV, London 1936-1940.
23. Leonard Forster, 'Tagwerk eines Hofmannes', Herbert Singer and Benno von Wiese, edd., *Festschrift für Richard Alewyn*, Berlin 1967, p. 103 ff.

24. J. S. Smart, *The Sonnets of Milton*, Glasgow 1921, p. 118. The
    translations of Milton's Italian poems quoted in the text are taken
    from this work (now reprinted in paperback, Oxford 1966).
25. By Odette de Mourgues; see her *Metaphysical, Baroque and Précieux
    Poetry*, Oxford 1953, p. 115 ff, and *La Fontaine's Fables*, London
    1960, p. 14 ff. The term 'lyrical Esperanto' was coined by Gustav
    René Hocke, *Manierismus in der Literatur*, Rowohlts deutsche
    Enzyklopädie, Hamburg 1959, p. 114.
26. Hugo von Hofmannsthal, 'Das Buch von Peter Altenberg', *Die
    prosaischen Schriften gesammelt*, Berlin 1907, II, p. 7; Peter Alten-
    berg, *Wie ich es sehe*, 4. Aufl. Berlin 1904, p. 59.

4 Stefan George and R. M. Rilke

Verse written in foreign languages as a five-finger exercise is usually, though not always, the work of young poets, who are developing their own style by acquiring an existing style in the foreign language. So it is that poetry of this kind is often rather old-fashioned for its date. We saw how Van der Noot simply took over the established diction of the Pléiade. Weckherlin's English verses, with the one exception I considered before, look back to Spenser; he writes as though Shakespeare and his contemporaries had never lived, whereas his German verses are extremely modern; his French verses are a good deal less modern, but not so old-fashioned as his English ones. The French verse written by Constantijn Huygens as a young man was very up to date, but he was unable to keep pace with the developments in France, so that his later poems, though quite as accomplished, probably seemed rather provincial to Parisian ears. Milton's Italian poetry has received high praise from Italian critics, including the scholarly poet Giosuè Carducci[1]—no mean judge—but it is in the style of the late sixteenth century; for instance the new development undertaken by Marino thirty-five years before Milton was writing had no influence on him at all. By Italian standards Milton was nearly fifty years out of date.

There remains the other aspect of polyglot writing, the use of the proper language for given purposes. It is still operating today in certain spheres; we are not surprised to find menus written in French and directions on musical scores in Italian. As the seventeenth century advanced, French began to supersede Latin as the *lingua franca* of cultured intercourse, and George I of England, fresh from Hanover, spoke French with his English ministers. Leibniz published his philosophical work directed at a European public in Latin, but also, increasingly, in French; his writings in German were of local interest only. The view of languages as material to be used as expedient still subsisted throughout the eighteenth century. For Frederick the Great French was the vehicle of culture, a European medium more up to date than Latin, the language of the great world: for the ruler of a backward, impoverished and obscure state in Eastern Europe it was a means of contact for himself and his people with that great world, and so he surrounded himself with French intellectuals and wrote extensively in French. In Russia, an even more backward state, even further east, this remained true until 1917; educated Russians were proficient in French and the nobility even spoke it among themselves.[2] Russian novels of the great period, in the nineteenth century, sometimes have long passages of dialogue— between Russian aristocrats—in French. But Latin still carried special prestige. Dr Johnson thought in 1773 that Latin was the only fit vehicle for 'everything intended to be universal and permanent' and maintained stoutly in 1776 that 'he would never consent to disgrace the walls of Westminster Abbey with an English inscription'.[3] Even in later years Latin has held its own as a neutral language; the joint monument to Wolfe and Montcalm on the Plains of Abraham at Quebec bears the moving legend: 'Mortem virtus communem, famam historia, monumentum posteritas dedit.' It was erected in 1827 by a Scottish Governor, Lord Dalhousie, whose record in Quebec in other respects was not a happy one; the classical tradition in which he had been brought up was stronger in Scotland than in England, and the consummate tact which his use of Latin in this case displays has been notably lacking in Canadian politics since his day—perhaps in part because of the lack of a supra-national linguistic vehicle which he was still able to use. Even in our own day the coins of the multilingual Swiss Confederation bear the legend 'Confoederatio

Helvetica', not 'Schweiz Suisse Svizzera'. Some years ago the University College of North Wales at Bangor built a new hall of residence for students, Neuadd Reichel; it was named in memory of the first Principal of the College who, it so happened, was an Irishman of German ancestry. There is an inscription commemorating the opening of the building; it is in Welsh and Latin. The true function of the Latin is to avoid the use of English in a centre of Welsh nationalism, but ostensibly it is to allude discreetly to the circumstance that the man whose name the building bears was neither Welsh nor English. Latin still has its uses in bilingual societies.

In the eighteenth century the letter was an art form in a way it is not now. It was thought natural enough that Horace Walpole should conduct his correspondence with Madame du Deffand—no mean judge in such matters—entirely in French and that it should be able to withstand her critical eye. Goethe as a student at Leipzig exercised himself almost as a matter of course in writing not only letters but also verses in French and even in English, of which these are a specimen:[4]

> What pleasure, God! of like a flame to born,
> A virteous fire, that n'er to vice can turn,
> What volupty! when trembling in my arms,
> The bosom of my maid my bosom warmeth!
> Perpetual kisses of her lips o'erflow,
> In holy embrace mighty virtue show.
> When I then, rapt, in never felt extase,
> My maid! I say, and she, my dearest! says,
> When then, my heart, of love and virtue hot,
> Cries: come ye angels! Come! See and envy me not.

While still at school he and his sister had planned a polyglot novel. The various languages were the vehicle of the essentially cosmopolitan culture of the time. This was especially true of French; in 1765 Boswell went to Holland primarily to study law and to improve his French, not to learn Dutch, and Goethe went to Strasbourg in 1770 partly in order to improve his knowledge of French and doubtless with its aid to take some part in the bilingual literary life of that bicultural city. He was induced to give up this idea by his experiences in French-speaking circles there. He found in full sway the rigid ideals of *raison, vraisemblance, bon goût, clarté, style noble, élégance,* from which Parisians were beginning to free themselves (though they did not entirely succeed until 1830); and even in Paris it was still possible for the Maréchale de Luxembourg to cast a daring glance into the Bible and observe, shuddering, 'Ah Madame, quel dommage que le Saint Esprit eût aussi peu de goût'.[5] Originality of expression, towards which Goethe's own poetic development was leading him, based in part at least on the language of the Bible, appeared to his French friends as plain incompetence in the handling of the foreign language. As a result, to the great benefit of German literature, he decided to give up the unequal struggle. The young Goethe was one of many who have fallen a victim to the myth of the Genius of the French Language. At this point it is perhaps sufficient to suggest that what this much used phrase really designates is a certain pedestrian absence of genius in the French Academy. It is interesting to see Goethe's initial readiness; for people of his generation the various languages were still the vehicles of a European culture. Even thirty years later August Wilhelm Schlegel (admittedly under the influence of Madame de Staël) wrote an important part of his critical work in French.[6] But, thanks in part to Goethe's friend Herder, the climate was changing. Two examples, a hundred years apart, may serve to make this clear.

In 1784 William Beckford wrote his oriental fantasy *Vathek* in French. No one thought that there was anything odd in an English merchant turned country gentleman writing a novel in French, least of all anything disgraceful. It was certainly no odder than many of the eccentric things that Beckford did, and a good deal less odd than some of them. In 1894 Oscar Wilde wrote *Salomé* in French; this was thought to be a scandal. Language loyalty had supervened. The change can be further illustrated by two anecdotes from everyday life.

'My grandfather,' wrote Lytton Strachey in 1928,[7] 'an Anglo-Indian of cultivation and intelligence, once accompanied Carlyle on an excursion to Paris in pre-railroad days. At their destination the postilion asked my grandfather for a tip; but the reply—it is Carlyle who tells the story—was a curt refusal, followed by the words: "Vous avez drivé devilish slow." The reckless insularity of this remark,' Strachey goes on, 'illustrates well enough the extraordinary change which had come over the English governing classes since the eighteenth century. Fifty years earlier a cultivated Englishman would have piqued himself upon answering the postilion in the idiom and accent of Paris.' I can adduce a parallel anecdote, as it were in reverse.

My godfather[8] was a consultant physician who after taking a first degree at Glasgow did his clinical work at the Sorbonne and acquired there an excellent command of French, which he retained to the end of his life. One day about the beginning of this century (perhaps ten years after the appearance of *Salomé*, the author of which he knew personally), he was walking down Regent Street in company with a medical colleague, and was stopped by a young Frenchman inquiring the way in very broken English. The information needed was complicated, so my godfather explained in French, whereupon the pair continued down Regent Street in silence, finally broken by the medical colleague, who said, without a flicker: 'Well, Williams, I have always thought that you were a profoundly immoral man, and now I am convinced of it.' Fluent knowledge of French could only have been acquired in the course of a presumably vicious life in Paris.

What had happened to bring about this change of attitude? Strachey lists 'the Napoleonic wars, the industrial revolution, the Romantic revival, the Victorian spirit' and doubtless there were other causes too, but for the sake of simplicity and brevity it would be best to concentrate on one only—the Romantic revival.

In the meantime the Romantics had discovered that languages had souls, that each language, nay each dialect, was unique and characteristic; and this discovery had been utilized by the rising forces of nationalism. The energies of writers were devoted to the production of 'national literature'. If, like the Swiss Conrad Ferdinand Meyer, you had two languages at your disposal as artistic media, your choice between them was determined by your emotional or even your political allegiance. Meyer finally decided to write in German as a result of the war of 1870 and the unification of Germany—not a very good reason, we may now think, especially for a Swiss; until then he had seriously considered writing in French. Cases of writers changing from one language to another for similar but opposite reasons have been very numerous since 1933; I will mention only two: the Alsatian author René Schickele, who so far had written entirely in German, left Germany in 1933 and in 1938 just before his death published his only work in French, *Le retour*—the 'return' to the language of his childhood. Arthur Koestler, since his emigration, has written exclusively in English. The case of Joseph Conrad is a striking one, though it has little to do with politics and more with English as the international *lingua franca* of seamen. For Rilke political considerations played no part, yet his French poems are a profession of attachment—attachment not so much to French culture as to the Canton Valais where his last happy years were spent. By contrast, his contemporary Stefan George stands closer to Renaissance and Baroque practice with his verses in French and English.

What George sought was discipline, concentration and symbolic statement. He grew up in the period of Naturalism, which seemed to him to preach banality and indiscipline. Formal perfection was for him both a means to discipline and an expression of it. The way to formal perfection was through extensive experimentation. He was gifted for languages; he learnt Greek, Latin, French and English at school, to which he later added Spanish, Italian, Dutch, Polish and Norwegian—this last in order to read Ibsen in the original. His cultural world was that of Western European Latin Christendom; the Slavonic and Greek Orthodox worlds lay outside his field of interest. (The Poles he reckoned as Western Europeans because they were Catholics.) The rejuvenation of German poetry at which he aimed was to be built on the broadest and deepest cultural foundations. As he experimented with forms, so he experimented with languages, doubtless in order to get away from the associations of the German poetic idiom which he had inherited. Not content with existing languages, having their own poetic diction, which carried its own associations, he invented two languages of his own, and wrote poetry in both of them. One he called 'lingua romana'; it was largely based on Spanish, and he included three poems written in it in his collected works. The other was a 'mythical' language, and only two lines of it are still extant. The two languages evidently reflected two aspects of civilization: the Latin European world and the primitive mythical one, in both of which he felt that German poetry should be rooted. The construction of personal, previously non-existent, languages—and not just one but two—for the express purpose of writing poetry in them, is an extreme case. It is particularly interesting because these languages are obviously considered as material for the artist, not as means of communication. It is not difficult to understand the 'lingua romana', and George obviously reckoned with this when he allowed the two poems in it to be published, from one of which the following extract is taken:

> La sera vola circa me con alas taciturnas.
> El di ha pasato con suo violento túrben
> Suo furioso e insaciable ager.
> En veloz e insana capcia
> Se precipitaron copiosamente meas ideas
> Las unas devorando las altras. [. . .]

Indeed at an early date he described it[9] as 'eine ebenso klingende wie leicht verständliche literatursprache für meinen eigenen bedarf' (a literary language for my own use, as sonorous as it is comprehensible). The mythical language however remains hermetic, and the story goes that George translated the first book of the *Odyssey* into it, but caused the translation to be destroyed before his death in order to prevent prying philologists from reconstructing the language.[10] The two lines which we possess of it come at the end of a German poem entitled *Urspruenge* (Origins), much like the early Spanish *harğa* at the end of a *muwaššaha*, and create by their sonority, their strangeness, and not least by their incomprehensibility the effect of primitive utterance; the poem shows how, alongside the asceticism of the early church, an earlier form of existence persisted:

> Doch an dem flusse im schilfpalaste
> Trieb uns der wollust erhabenster schwall:
> In einem sange den keiner erfasste
> Waren wir heischer und herrscher vom All.
> Süss und befeuernd wie Attikas choros
> Über die hügel und inseln klang:
> CO BESOSO PASOJE PTOROS
> CO ES ON HAMA PASOJE BOAÑ.

> . . . In incantations which none comprehended
> We were the sovereign and ruled the All.
> Sweet and impelling as Atticas chorus
> Over the islands and hills we sang:[11]
> . . . . .

A man who goes to these lengths to exercise himself in an untried medium may be expected to do the same in existing languages too. We know that he did so to a quite considerable extent, though all we have are four poems in French and two in English. He made his own translations of all of them, which he incorporated in his various volumes of poetry. Some of the originals were published in the final volume of his collected works, which did not appear until after his death, as specimens of what one must suppose to have been a fair number of poems in foreign languages which formed preliminary stages of poems still only accessible to us in German. The appendix to the third volume of the collected works, which appeared before George's death, had hinted at the existence of such poems and included an interesting defence of the practice of writing in foreign languages: 'Das dichten in fremdem sprachstoff, das der laie leicht für spielerische laune nehmen kann, hat aber seine notwendigkeit. In der fremden sprache in der er fühlt sich bewegt und denkt fügen sich dem Dichter die klänge ähnlich wie in der muttersprache' (Creative writing in a foreign linguistic vehicle, which the layman is liable to consider mere playful fancy, has a necessity of its own. In the foreign language in which he feels, moves and thinks, the sounds join together for the Poet in the same way as in his mother tongue). This refers to the inner process of creation, the way 'the sounds join together' in the poet's mind. In a following passage the point is made that though literary influences were not absent, the composition of poetry in foreign languages was firmly anchored in the poet's practical use of these languages—French in his lengthy stays in Paris and Brussels, Spanish with Spanish friends in Berlin, English as a result of his friendship with the young English composer Cyril Scott, also in Berlin and Frankfurt;[12] and the writer goes on to point out that some Italian verses were included in German translation in another volume of poems.

It would seem that George wished to convey the impression that writing poetry in foreign languages was not just a game, but that it was justified for him by the social circumstances of his own life, and that the creative process involved was no different from that which obtained in his mother tongue. There is no mention of stylistic exercise, or of the use such writing could have for the development of poetry in German, yet there can be no doubt that this was his primary purpose, otherwise it is difficult to see why he did not publish these works in the original. The parallel with Weckherlin is close. In his case his work in English and French was published at the command of his prince. As soon as his circumstances changed and he was able to please himself, he published exclusively in German. Though, as we know, he continued to write in Latin, English and French, it was only the German versions that he published, and he did not reprint any of his early foreign language publications in his collected works in 1648. Polyglot though George was, he had no ambition to be regarded as a polyglot poet, and it is difficult to estimate how many of his early German poems are based on work originally written in some other language. He saw his mission in the reform of German poetry, and everything else was subordinated to that.

There had been moments when his courage had failed him and he had considered writing entirely in French. But he realized that this, however difficult, would be a too easy way out. It was taken by others of his own epoch—the Greek Jean Moréas, the Americans Stuart Merrill and Francis Viélé-Griffin and other obscurer figures now forgotten, all of whom were more firmly rooted in France by parentage or upbringing than George was. His friends, both German and French, did their best to dissuade him. His French mentor, the symbolist poet Albert Saint-Paul (one of those fortunate hotel acquaintanceships which sometimes fall to the lot of the intelligent young), who had introduced him to Mallarmé, wrote later of how George had dreaded his return to Germany: 'Il hésitait à faire ce voyage et se décidait presque à écrire en français et à rester à Paris. Il composa même quelques poèmes en notre langue. Je l'en dissuadais cependant, convaincu que son œuvre devait être allemande. Je lui affirmais qu'il serait le maître du renouveau de la poésie lyrique dans son pays.' His German friend Carl August Klein exerted, as he said, 'all his influence' in the same direction.[13] And so George was won for German literature by resisting an insidious temptation. The first line of the famous poem *Franken* in *Der siebente Ring,* in which he speaks of what he owed to French culture, may well refer to this temptation: 'Es war am schlimmsten kreuzweg meiner fahrt.' On his return to Germany he felt so isolated and repelled by the literature of the time that he elaborated his 'lingua romana'; he wrote to a friend that he had written nothing for some time, 'weil ich einfach nicht weiss in welcher sprache ich schreiben soll' (because I simply do not know in which language I ought to write).[14] The temptation was not easy to resist, and one of the ways of resisting it was to make it work in the service of the new kind of German poetry that George aimed to create.

Looking back from where we now stand, we may try to judge just how insidious this temptation was by assessing George as a French poet on the basis of the very few French poems of his that we have. This was done, more than thirty years ago, by Hans Jaeger, and as no one has since reopened the question, his results still hold the field. He finds[15] that George's poems have true poetic quality and communicate something peculiar to the poet, i.e. that they are not mere imitation or pastiche, that they are linguistically correct, free from Germanisms in idiom or diction, and even that they contain lines which a Frenchman might have been glad to have written—e.g. 'Je sens le doigt paisible de la mort' (*Frauenlob*).

We may perhaps be able to gather from these four poems[16] what George's contribution to French poetry might have been like.

One of them deals with a fairy-tale theme from a world combined of Grimm and an idealized Germanic middle age, and bears the significant title *Variations sur thèmes germaniques;* another is called *Frauenlob,* referring to a medieval poet whose legend-encrusted life was familiar in Germany, but whose very name would have been exotic and unknown in France. The third, *Proverbes,* is a piece of wise advice to three friends—the Belgian poets Paul Gérardy, Edmond Rassenfosse and Léon Paschal, together with whom he had spent a weekend in 1895:

Proverbes: *pour les trois invités de Sur-le-Mont* T[ilff]

Pendant que ta mère t'allaite
Il faut qu'une fée maligne
Chante d'ombre et de mort.
Elle te donne comme étrennes
Ces yeux sinistres et si mornes
Et dont les Muses s'éprennent.

Quand tes frères se plaignent
Et disent: ô ma douleur! la tienne
Ne la dis qu'aux nuages la nuit—
Et tes chairs d'enfant saignent
Sous l'arme dure des doigts.

Sache que tu dois
Tuer ta fraîche jeunesse·
Car ce n'est que sur son tombeau—
Si bien des pleurs l'arrosent—qu'éclosent
Parmi la seule flore merveilleuse
Les seules belles roses.

'En nous quittant,' writes Paschal, 'il laissa, un peu en guise d'adieu et de souvenir, un petit poème français, dont la première strophe était dédiée à Gérardy, la deuxième à Rassenfosse et la troisième à moi'[17] and in which in each verse he struck the note appropriate to the recipient. It is George's French *art poétique.* The whole poem preaches—the word is not too strong—the twenty-three-year-old poet's personal gospel of self-discipline in the service of poetry to come. This gospel—in a French context—if applied to questions of form, would seem to lead back to the Parnassians, though what George doubtless had in mind was Mallarmé's devotion to his art, which he later commemorated in the admiring line:

Und für sein denkbild blutend—MALLARMÉ.

The last, *D'une Veillée*, is a successful combination of George's power of visual evocation with the fluidity of which the French symbolists were masters, extending even to the use of a colloquialism like 'ne joue pas avec' which he would never have permitted himself in German:

> Ton front mi-couvert d'une nuée de cheveux
> (Ils sont blonds et soyeux)
> Ton front me dit les combats juvéniles.
> Tes lèvres (elles sont muettes) content le drame
> Des âmes que Dieu condamne.
> Emouvant miroir· tes yeux!
> Ne joue pas avec! il est fragile . .
> Même quand tu souris (enfin tu t'es endormie)
> Ce sourire est mélancholie
> Et tu penches un peu ta tête endolorie.

George could thus have made a personal contribution by the treatment of specifically German subjects in French; by disciplined devotion to a symbolist ideal of poetry; and by exploiting his visual gift. He would not have been the only poet writing in French to do so. Morover it is doubtful whether by just gritting his teeth or clenching his fists till they bled—

> Et tes chairs d'enfant saignent
> Sous l'arme dure des doigts

—he would have reached the stature which his sense of mission enabled him to achieve in German. He would have had the consolation of being a member of a movement, of the fellowship in common craftsmanship and common endeavour, as, looking back, he remembered nostalgically how in Paris 'umgab mich jugend Im taumel aller dinge die mir teuer' (youth was all about me, carried away by all the things I cherish), but one cannot see him doing more than eventually forming a little cénacle round himself in Paris, with young men addressing him as 'cher maître'; its influence would have been restricted and in no way to be compared with the effect he actually produced on generations of German youth, commanding and inspiring by his very isolation.

> Mag traum und ferne uns als speise stärken—
> Luft die wir atmen bringt nur der Lebendige.

Though dream and distance give us strength and nurture,
Air that we breathe the living only proffer.[18]

George's English poems have received some rough treatment
from Ralph Farrell,[19] rougher I think than they deserve. We have
only two of them, but, as Farrell observes, the general competence
they show in the handling of English presupposes a good deal of
earlier practice in writing English verse. Like his French poems
they are linguistically and technically correct, and though they
have little originality they show a good deal of skill in exploiting
the sonorous diction elaborated by Rossetti and Swinburne, both
of whom George admired and translated. Farrell was writing over
thirty years ago, and the renewed taste for Victorian literature
which has come up in recent years suggests a less harsh judgement
than his. There were plenty of minor English poets at the turn
of the century who wrote worse verses than these:

> You boldly ceased to love the God of yore·
> Now he appears with dark revengeful brow:
> 'You who called servitude my precious lore
> And left my house too proud to make the bow,
>   Are you not bent by a more shameful yoke
> Do you not feel your wrung arm's force decay
> More than by this sonorous chain you broke?
> Must you not cry for pity· watch and pray?'
>   Yea! as I neared the Saviour's bloody feet
> I now exalt a new God whom I greet
> With quivering lips· and equal extasies
> Consume me, and less sober sympathies,
> When last light of the holy evening wanes
> In my cathedral's gold and purple panes.

George's French poetry is not pastiche; his English verses, skilled
as they are, cannot really be called anything else. His German
translations of them are in a different category. When Cyril
Scott, to whom these poems were addressed, published a volume
of translations from George, he put George's German version of
one of them back into English. The result was apparently totally
different and seems not to have received the approval of the
Master.[20]

George's work in foreign languages was thus workshop practice, used ultimately in the service of his German poetry, and it
all dates from early in his career. The temptation to write in
French seems to have been the result less of an allegiance to
French culture than of an aversion from the German literature of
his day.

The case of Rilke is very different. His early workshop practice was done in German, and he published it. It has since alas been reprinted, and it may serve as an example of what lamentably bad poetry a great poet can write before he finds his feet. But Rilke's wrestling with poetry—as much with the problem of what to say as of how to say it—is impressive and compels admiration. Foreign languages have little to do with it. Yet his collected works contain poems in Italian, in Russian, and above all in French.[21] The Italian verses may be dealt with summarily, for they cannot really be taken seriously, and indeed Rilke himself never published them. They consist of two poems, together making up a mere fourteen lines. The first poem breaks off after four lines, which contain one grammatical error and one metrical infelicity. The remaining ten lines of unrhymed free verse give an Italian reformulation of the more revolting kind of early Rilkean sentimentality about little birds, angels, sleeping children and, inevitably, the poet's soul. They are a mere fleeting exercise, and nothing seems to be known of any biographical circumstances which could justify their production, let alone their publication. There is no hint of practice or preparation for his work in German; on the contrary. And there is no sense of allegiance in them to Italian culture or the Italian landscape.

But Rilke was a man of strong allegiances, and one of them was to Russia. It was a highly idealized Russia, compounded of the virtues of simplicity, spirituality and poverty which Rilke felt were embodied in wide open spaces, saintly monks and poor peasants. His first visit to Moscow in 1899 coincided with Easter, and reinforced his preconceived ideas. 'When I first came to Moscow,' he later said, 'everything seemed familiar and known from of old. It was at Eastertime, and it moved me as if it were my Easter, my spring, my bells. It was the city of my oldest and deepest memories; it was a continual recognition and greeting: it was home'.[22] After five weeks in Russia he returned to Germany and together with Lou Andreas-Salomé worked hard at Russian. By the middle of March 1900 he could read the great Russian writers in the original 'without much trouble', and in May he visited Russia again. There he lived for three days as a peasant among peasants—savouring the primitiveness of their existence. Rilke had fallen in love with the great Russian soul, and this love expressed itself in the first part of *Das Stundenbuch,* the 'book of monkish life', and the *Geschichten vom lieben Gott.* Rilke was fond of emphasising his affinity for all things Russian, and even told Charles du Bos[23] that he had at one time contemplated giving up German altogether and writing entirely in Russian. It is reasonable to inquire about his proficiency in the language. He had studied it intensively for two months, and had spent about six months in all in the country. Gifted though he was, his knowledge can have been neither wide nor deep. The eight Russian poems we have were all written after his return from Russia; they were addressed to Lou Andreas-Salomé, from whom he had learnt Russian and who had travelled in Russia with him. She personified his contact with the country, and the poems arise out of a feeling of nostalgia. He sent her one of them with a note—in German—explaining that he had written it amid the hubbub of a Berlin café, evoking a ride he and she had taken by night in Russia. Stefan George (or his spokesman) had made the point that the 'sounds join together' for the poet in the same way, whether the language he uses is his mother-tongue or not. But in the foreign language the poet can only join the sounds he has got in the way which he knows, and that is not always the right way. Some attention has been given to these poems,[24] and as I know no Russian I must go by what competent scholars have pointed out. Rilke's Russian is incorrect in grammar, syntax and idiom, and as he seems not to have grasped the rules of Russian accentuation many of his lines do not scan properly. His Russian poems have the same effect on a Russian that Goethe's English verses have on us, and for much the same reason. There is general agreement that these verses show poetic quality but no linguistic mastery, and that Rilke has not succeeded in saying anything in them which he could not equally well have said in German. Rilke's dissatisfaction with German, which he did know, and his preference for Russian, which he did not, has been well explained, in part at least, by his feeling of 'the absolute inadequacy of all language';[25] he was not alone in feeling this, and the classic expression of it in German literature is by Hugo von Hofmannsthal—who wrote no poetry in any language but German.

Rilke's Russian verses show that allegiance by itself, however sincere, is not enough. His French verses are quite another matter. Unlike George's, they were written at the end of his life, when his chief works, the *Elegies* and the *Sonnets to Orpheus*, were already completed. They are in no sense training or preparation for anything. Rilke's French, like George's, was acquired, not native, but he had considerable control of the language and spoke and wrote it with some elegance, tempered with what

Léon-Paul Fargue called 'une gaucherie subtile' which lent it a peculiar charm to French ears.[26]

Living the last years of his life in the French-speaking country-side of the Valais, it was natural for Rilke to formulate thoughts in French. On his country walks these thoughts often took the form of verses. He liked to think that they came to him, as the *Elegies* and the *Sonnets* had done, 'sous une dictée intérieure, à laquelle je ne pouvais qu'obéir',[27] as he wrote to a Swiss acquaintance. This seems to be rather overdramatizing the situation, but there is no doubt that his creativity, which had risen to the pitch of frenzy[28] when he was writing the *Sonnets* and completing the *Elegies*, still continued. The poems succeed admirably in fixing fugitive impressions of landscape, fleeting emotions; there is no sense of sweep, of a great integrated structure, in them. They are linked by a sameness of themes; Rilke always saw the same view and regularly took the same walk from his home at the Château de Muzot, he regularly saw the same things; with the changing seasons and changing times of day they presented themselves to him quite literally in different lights. And so these momentary impressions, essentially isolated in themselves, combine to form a whole greater than the sum of its parts, made out of devotion to the Swiss landscape. The tone is muted, for Rilke is a tired man. Yet the resemblance to his German poetry is obvious; there is no question here of the French language influencing his writing by giving it a different direction. Rilke transfers, apparently without effort, his mature style from German into French—on a miniature scale, for the poems are all short ones. The Rilkean devices we know so well are there: lines so arranged that the little words which bear no stress in the sentence come to carry the rhyme in the verse, especially prepositions like 'for' and 'from'; the trick of expressing the concrete in terms of the abstract and the abstract in terms of the concrete; everyday hackneyed themes turned upside-down or looked at from a new surprising angle: all these characteristics of his German poetry are present in the French.[29] It is his personal style, and not even the much-invoked Genius of the French Language can make him write differently— or make him write French as well as he wrote German, or make him give up writing in German. Here is an example:

Souvenirs de Muzot, I

Nous vivons sur un ancien sol d'échange,
où tout se donne, tout se rend—,

mais notre cœur souvent échange l'Ange
contre la vanité d'un ciel absent.

Le pain naïf, l'outil de tous les jours,
l'intimité des choses familières,
qui n'est capable de les laisser pour
un peu de vide où l'envie prospère.

Mais même ce vide, si nous le tenons
bien contre nous, s'échauffe et s'anime,
et l'Ange, pour le rendre légitime,
l'entoure doucement d'un violon.

One of the basic problems for Rilke, as for every modern poet, was to find an adequate, personal and above all a fresh and unspoilt poetic diction. One of the solutions he found was the use of ordinary, 'non-poetic' words. This early poem is a programmatic statement:[30]

Die armen Worte, die im Alltag darben,
die unscheinbaren Worte, lieb ich so.
Aus meinen Festen schenk ich ihnen Farben,
da lächeln sie und werden langsam froh.
Ihr Wesen, das sie bang in sich bezwangen,
erneut sich deutlich, dass es jeder sieht;
sie sind noch niemals im Gesang gegangen,
und schauernd schreiten sie in meinem Lied.

I love the poor words, the inconspicuous words, which live in penury in the everyday world. I give them colours from my festivals; then they smile and gradually grow glad. Their essence, which they had anxiously held imprisoned within them, renews itself plainly, so that all can see; they had never moved in song, and trembling they step out in *my* poem.

One can see from these lines that Rilke is a great master of that particularly British accomplishment—the discreet self-deprecatory understatement which is so discreet that it produces the same effect as resounding self-congratulation. In spite of appearances, what remains in the mind is not the poor neglected words which are being helped to a new, rich life, but that it is Rilke who is helping them; and he is doing it not out of charity but for his own quite definite purpose of achieving a new personal diction.

The use of a foreign language affords a further possibility: the words are not burdened with irrelevant associations for the poet, they are fresh and pristine. This is their appeal, particularly for a poet who has his great work behind him, in which he has exploited the resources of his mother tongue to the full. And so it is understandable that the French word for the orchard which he sees from his window acquires a freshness and a personal significance for him which the German word no longer could. Rilke himself loved to point out that it was superior to the German word for an orchard, because the German word is a compound and the French one is not, and there is no doubt that *verger* is more euphonious than *Obstgarten*. Now that he has an orchard of his own, the word *verger* comes to stand for the vocabulary of the French language as a whole, which gives him a new means of expression for things which had long pre-occupied him; it is no chance that the first of the lyric cycles that he published in French should be called *Vergers*—orchards. The title poem, which as originally published stands at the centre of the cycle, is a sequence which begins as follows:

Verger I.

Peut-être que si j'ai osé t'écrire,
langue prêtée, c'était pour employer
ce nom rustique dont l'unique empire
me tourmentait depuis toujours: Verger.

Pauvre poète qui doit élire
pour dire tout ce que ce nom comprend,
un à-peu-près trop vague qui chavire,
ou pire: la clôture qui défend.

Verger: ô privilège d'une lyre
de pouvoir te nommer simplement;
nom sans pareil qui les abeilles attire,
nom qui respire et attend . . .

Nom clair qui cache le printemps antique,
tout aussi plein que transparent,
et qui dans ses syllabes symétriques
redouble tout et devient abondant.

The unfortunate poet in the second verse is Rilke in his capacity as a German writer, forced to use an approximation which fails of its effect or which may even act as a barrier to true comprehension—in fact the German word. French has the 'privilège d'une lyre de pouvoir te nommer simplement'. The technique is worth noting: this poem has 16 lines, but only 6 rhymes, and moreover the second verse has two internal rhymes in *ire*. It is clear that Rilke takes delight in playing with his new medium, his new lyre. These lines finish with the evocation of abundance

—the orchard is an aspect of God's plenty, in which the poet is to spend what he well knows will be the last years of his life. In another poem, beginning 'Puisque tout passe . . . ', this realization comes out very clearly:

> Chantons ce qui nous quitte
> avec amour et art;
> soyons plus vite
> que le rapide départ.

The fifth poem of the sequence reveals this premonition of death, and the questioning hope that something of him may have passed into the fruit of the orchard. He regards the orchard as a flock of sheep and himself a kind of shepherd of the trees; shepherds are proverbially peaceful people. Here too it is not too fanciful, I think, to find in the orchard itself (not merely the word) a symbol for the French language, into which the poet hopes that something of his tranquillity may have passed before it is time for him to die:

> *Verger V.*
>
> Ai-je des souvenirs, ai-je des espérances,
> en te regardant, mon verger?
> Tu te repais autour de moi, ô troupeau d'abondance
> et tu fais penser ton berger.
>
> Laisse-moi contempler au travers de tes branches
> la nuit qui va commencer.
> Tu as travaillé; pour moi c'était un dimanche,
> mon repos, m'a-t-il avancé?
>
> D'être berger, qu'y a-t-il de plus juste en somme?
> Se peut-il qu'un peu de ma paix
> aujourd'hui soit entrée doucement dans tes pommes?
> Car tu sais bien, je m'en vais . . .

The mention of the apples at the end evokes one of Rilke's favourite symbols. E. C. Mason says: 'He was a great apple-eater, apples had for him a symbolic, quasi-sacramental significance. It would be easy to write a study on "Rilke and the Apple" and to make of it a comprehensive interpretation of his personality, outlook and art'.[31] In such a study, which I cannot undertake here, this poem would have its place. But there are other aspects of it which are important for my purpose: the phrase 'pour moi c'était un dimanche' highlights the circumstance that Rilke's French poems are the work of a 'Sunday poet'—a satisfying hobby, but also *repose* from the exhausting work of his life. The pleasure he got from it comes out clearly in the letter to a Swiss acquaintance from which I have already quoted: 'C'est très étonnant de se trouver [...] "pratiquant" sur le sol d'une autre langue: que j'y étais jeune, il me semblait que tout recommence avec cet instrument nouveau et j'étais presque effrayé, mais d'une frayeur heureuse, de le sentir vibrer sous mon toucher timide, de plus en plus hardi.' It still seemed to him, even now that he was no longer so young, that everything started afresh with this new instrument: a consoling thought for a man who had done his life's work and who was living under the shadow of death. A year after writing this letter he was dead—at the early age of fifty-one.

If the choice of the language in which a poet writes is a declaration of allegiance, then it is clear that the allegiance which is expressed in Rilke's French verses is, as I suggested before, to the countryside of Canton Valais,[32] not to French culture as a whole. Rilke had been steeped in French culture for years. If he had wished to affirm his attachment to it by writing poetry in French he could have done so easily at any time. In fact we have scattered French verses of his from as early as 1899, but this thin trickle shows nothing of any consequence. They are minor pieces, like the Italian verses we have already noticed. For instance, there is one dating from 1902; it was not a gesture towards France, but towards Rodin, to whom he wrote: 'Pourquoi je vous écris ces vers? Non parce que j'ose croire qu'il sont bons [they are in fact very mediocre], mais c'est le désir de m'approcher de vous qui me guide la main.'[33] This is true of his other French verses before his last years in Switzerland; many of them are no more than the cunning fisherman's lure. The potentiality was there, but he did not exercise it for serious poetic creation until later. The world to which Rilke's French poetry, even at its best, expresses allegiance is a private world.

Rilke's case is different from any of the others we have considered so far, on several counts. In the first place there is his adoption of a different medium towards the end of his life, as relaxation rather than as training. Then there is the volume of work he wrote in it—it fills 230 pages in the new edition of his collected works—and the circumstance that some of it was actually published in France during his life-time. He was thus accepted as a French poet by the French literary world, and indeed it was no less a figure than Paul Valéry who encouraged him to continue writing in French and to get his work published in France.[34]

A Frenchman knowing no German who wanted to know what Rilke's poetry was like would get a very fair idea from reading his production in French. It would be deficient in a number of respects: he would not see Rilke as a poet of sweep and power capable of writing the *Duino Elegies* for instance; he would not be able to appreciate certain other sides of Rilke's work important to the German reader, particularly the wide range of themes and the elaboration of the 'Dinggedichte'; and he would not realize the extent to which Rilke had enriched the German language and extended the range of German poetic diction; he would see him as a meritorious follower of Valéry. He would be seeing a miniature Rilke, but on this smaller scale the general impression would be correct.

If the same man were to try the same procedure with Stefan George the result would be quite misleading. Not merely because of the small body of material (it is sometimes possible to form a reliable first impression of a poet's work from just one poem), but for two other reasons as well. In the first place because George's French verses are early and do not suggest the nature of his mature work, and in the second because of differences in the literary scene in France and Germany at the time George was writing. His French symbolist friends were concerned to loosen and render more flexible the rigid poetic diction they had inherited from the Parnassians. George saw clearly that German poetic diction was too slack, not to say sloppy, and that what was required was more rigour. If his French verses can stand on their own feet it is because he was using French as his French contemporaries were using it, not as he was later to use German. The poem *D'une veillée* is very characteristic in this respect.

An English reader in a similar position, with only the two English poems to judge from, would form a much more reliable impression, though they date from the same period of George's life as the French poems. The second one (quoted above) especially corresponds very closely in style to the poems of the *Teppich des Lebens* volume in which the German version appeared, particularly in the way in which it builds up to the symbolic visual image in the last line. But for any English reader since Eliot and Pound this is a period piece; he would see George as a minor Victorian poet and be left wondering how a man who wrote like this could still have a vital influence in Germany as late as his death in 1934 or even later, when English poets of the Victorian generations were largely forgotten. So the initially correct impression would be falsified by the different course and speed of change in literary taste in the two countries.

1. G. Carducci, *Primi Saggi*, Bologna 1889, p. 455 ff (= *Opere*, II). Carducci here discusses Louisa Grace and Thomas Matthias, who also wrote poetry in Italian. There is an interesting parallel in the case of the Portuguese poet Fernando Pessoa, who was born in South Africa and whose first published work was in English; see Georg Rudolf Lind and Ulrich Suerbaum, 'Dichten in fremden Sprachen. Zu bisher unveröffentlichten englischen Gedichten Fernando Pessoas', *Poetica*, II (1968) p. 237 ff., esp. p. 270-1.
2. The background to this is dealt with by André Mazon, *Deux Russes écrivains français*, Paris 1964.
3. *Tour to the Hebrides*, September 5, 1773 in J. Boswell, *Life of Johnson*, ed. G. Birkbeck Hill, Oxford 1887 ff, V, p. 154; *Life of Johnson*, June 1776 ed. cit. III, p. 83-84, and other similar utterances by Johnson in the notes (on the subject of his epitaph for Oliver Goldsmith).
4. Goethe's verses in foreign languages are included in the *complete* editions of his poetry, e.g. the Insel edition *Goethes Gedichte in zeitlicher Folge*, ed. Hans Gerhard Gräf. Richard Friedenthal produced a privately printed edition of *Goethes englische Werke* in 1961 (Westerham Press, Westerham, Kent, 500 copies only). The poem quoted will be found in the volume devoted to Goethe in *The Penguin Poets* series, edited by David Luke, Harmondsworth 1964, p. 4.
5. Quoted by Lytton Strachey in his essay 'Madame du Deffand', *Collected Works Biographical Essays*, London 1948, p. 173.
6. A. W. Schlegel, *Essais littéraires et historiques*, Bonn 1842; *Œuvres écrites en français*, ed. E. Böcking, Leipzig 1846.
7. Lytton Strachey, *Collected Works, Biographical Essays*, London 1948, p. 245.
8. Leonard Llewellyn Bulkeley Williams; see *Who was Who 1929-1940*, London 1941, p. 1461; *The Lancet*, CCXXXVII part II (July-December 1939) pp. 579, 715.
9. Quoted by Franz Schonauer, *Stefan George in Selbstzeugnissen und Bilddokumenten*, Hamburg (Rororo) 1960, p. 24. The texts of the two poems in 'lingua romana' are printed in the *Schlussband* of George's collected works, p. 130 ff.
10. Ernst Morwitz, *Kommentar zu den Prosa- Drama- und Jugend-Dichtungen Stefan Georges*, Munich 1962, p. 290. George himself wrote in a different context: 'Jeden wahren künstler hat einmal die sehnsucht befallen in einer sprache sich auszudrücken deren die unheilige menge sich nie bedienen würde', *Tage und Taten*, p. 53.
11. Translation by Ulrich K. Goldsmith, *Stefan George: a Study of his Early Work*, Boulder, Colorado 1959, p. 16. Other verse translations are taken from the complete version by Olga Marx and Ernst Morwitz, *The Works of Stefan George*, Chapel Hill 1949.
12. And, as now appears, with the English musician Clement Harris in the same years; C. V. Bock, 'Stefan George and Clement Harris', *Modern Language Review* LXIII (1968) p. 897 ff.
13. Quoted by Hans Jaeger, 'Stefan Georges französische Gedichte und deutsche Übertragungen', *Publications of the Modern Language Association* LI (1936) p. 580.

14. Schonauer, op. cit., p. 24.
15. Hans Jaeger, op. cit., p. 592.
16. Texts in the *Schlussband*, p. 132 ff.
17. Quoted by Enid Lowry Duthie, *L'influence du symbolisme français dans le renouveau poétique de l'Allemagne: les Blätter für die Kunst de 1892 à 1900*, Paris 1933, p. 306 and by Jaeger, p. 588.
18. Both quotations are from the poem 'Franken' in *Der siebente Ring*, p. 19.
19. Ralph Farrell, *Stefan Georges Beziehungen zur englischen Dichtung*, Berlin 1937 (= *Germanische Studien* 192), p. 218 ff.
20. Both of the English poems printed in the *Schlussband* of the collected works, pp. 136-7, are translated in *Der Teppich des Lebens*, where they form part of the cycle of three poems entitled 'Ein knabe der mir von herbst und abend sang' dedicated to Cyril Scott. The third poem in this cycle, which was presumably also originally written in English, was translated by Cyril Scott in his *Stefan George: Selection from his Works translated into English*, London 1910, p. 41. It was doubtless for this reason that the English original was not printed in the *Schlussband* in 1934.
21. Rilke, *Sämtliche Werke*, ed. Ernst Zinn, Inselverlag 1955 ff, contains the French and Italian poems in volume II, the Russian poems in vol. IV.
22. Rilke to Ellen Key, 2 April 1904, quoted by E. M. Butler, *Rainer Maria Rilke*, Cambridge 1941, p. 50. Her comments on Rilke's Russian experiences are characteristically clear-headed and sensible.
23. Charles du Bos, in the collective volume *Rilke et la France*, Paris 1942, p. 211.
24. Samson Soloveitchik and E. B. Gladding, 'Rilke's Original Russian Poems', *Modern Language Notes* LXII (1947) p. 514 ff. I am grateful to Dr N. Zissermann for kind help and for information about the impression these poems make on a Russian reader.
25. E. C. Mason, *Rilke, Europe, and the English-speaking World*, Cambridge 1961, p. 20-21. See also F. W. Wodtke, 'Das Problem der Sprache beim späten Rilke', *Orbis Litterarum* XI (1956), p. 64 ff, who comments on Rilke's use of French, esp. p. 105.
26. *Rilke et la France*, op. 221; E. C. Mason, op. cit., p. 209; K. A. J. Battersby, *Rilke and France: a Study in Poetic Development*, Oxford 1966, does not deal with Rilke's French poetry. By contrast, Hartmann Goertz, *Frankreich und das Erlebnis der Form im Werke Rainer Maria Rilkes*, Stuttgart 1932, has a valuable chapter on the subject.
27. To Madame Renée Favre, 18 November 1925, published by P.-E. Schazmann, *Gazette de Lausanne*, 5.i.1941. This important letter seems not to have been reprinted and has thus escaped the attention of scholars.
28. Perhaps 'frenzy' is an over-statement. It is a part of the Rilke legend which even E. M. Butler (op. cit., p. 318) was willing to accept. Maurice Zermatten, *Les années valaisannes de Rilke*, Sierre 1951, p. 94, points out that Rilke's housekeeper noticed nothing unusual in his behaviour during those weeks in February 1922 when he felt himself to be issuing vast commands to the universe, unable to think of food or rest.
29. For instance, in the poem quoted, *Souvenirs de Muzot I*, the non-concrete is treated as concrete:

> Mais même ce vide, si nous le tenons
> bien contre nous, s'échauffe et s'anime,

and the concrete violin is divested of its concreteness and becomes a sort of fluid violin-shaped line; the rhyme *jours-pour* is very Rilkean, as is the jingle *échange l'Ange*. The concentration of fugitive impressions in Rilke's French verses is allied to that in the Japanese *haiku* which he much admired and of which he sent copies to Sophie Giauque on 26 November 1925; Daniel Simond, ed., *Rilke en Valais,* Lausanne 1946, p. 83 ff.

30. *Sämtliche Werke,* I, p. 148.
31. E. C. Mason, op. cit., p. 242.
32. 'Dieses Wallis (: ja, wieso nennt man's nicht, wenn man die berühmtesten Gegenden der Erde aufzählt?) ist eine unvergleichliche Landschaft; erst erfasst' ich's noch nicht in Wahrheit, weil ich's verglich: [...] aber erst seit ich's ganz um seiner selbst willen anstaune, offenbart es mir seine grossen Verhältnisse und in ihnen, nach und nach erkennbar, die süsseste Anmut und die stärkste, inständigste Überlieferung'. Rilke to Gertrud Ouckama Knoop, 26 November 1921, *Briefe aus Muzot 1921-1926,* Leipzig 1935, p. 44. See also Maurice Zermatten, op. cit., passim and René Morax in *Rilke en Valais,* p. 23.
33. R. M. Rilke, *Lettres à Rodin,* ed. Georges Grappe, Paris 1931, p. 16.
34. *Rilke et la France,* pp. 210, 226.

5 James Joyce, Dadaism Surrealism and After

Stefan George, who paid great attention to the structural cohesion and unity of his published work, did not disdain to include in his poems lines in other languages than German, and even to place them in positions of emphasis at the end of the poem, where they form a climax. We saw how he did this with the couplet in his secret 'mythical' language in the poem *Urspruenge*. In the poem *Franken*, where he deals with what he owed to French culture, the culminating last line is a quotation from the *Chanson de Roland:* 'Returnent franc en France dulce terre'. He made only sporadic use of polyglot quotation as a stylistic device, as a means of evoking associations which draw on a wide cultural background, against which the poem is to be placed.

The two poets who developed this possibility and made it an element of their personal style were Ezra Pound and T. S. Eliot, and the way they used it is generally familiar. They aimed at 'presenting [. . .] graspable ideograms of entire cultures, motivations and sensibilities' by this means.[1] They make no real concession to the culturally underprivileged (despite Eliot's notes on *The Waste Land*). Hugh Kenner, after listing the foreign languages used by Pound in the *Cantos*—Latin, Greek, French, German, Italian, Chinese, Spanish, Provençal—goes on consolingly 'One need not know them all, though in this as in other matters the more one knows the sharper one's apprehension'.[2] There is a sense in which all this is merely a heightened version of a certain kind of egghead conversation among polyglots; the result is polyglot poetry, in which several different languages are used to form the texture of the poem. The best-known example is at the end of Eliot's *Waste Land*, where into seven lines of verse he packs in phrases from Dante, the Latin *Pervigilium Veneris*, Gérard de Nerval and the Upanishads.

Eliot, like George, had done his apprenticeship writing French verse, and like Milton (though he would object to the parallel) he had included it quite naturally in his published work. His four poems in French are successful practice pieces, much influenced by Jules Laforgue.[3] Two are flippant and amusing trifles, the others more serious. The only one which uses French to produce effects which would not be possible in English is *Le Directeur*, which exploits rhymes not available in English. The two serious pieces, *Lune de Miel* and *Dans le Restaurant*, are more accomplished. They are 'observations' like the poems in *Prufrock* and indeed date from the same time. The picture of the miserable Europe-trotting honeymoon couple, wrestling with bedbugs and blind to the cultural glories of Italy—or indeed anywhere else—is a piece of concentrated observation, and the contrast between the sordidness and transitoriness of present-day life and the nobility and permanence of the art of the past is one of the basic themes of Eliot's early work. In *Dans le Restaurant*, another 'observation', in which a garrulous old waiter regales a defenceless customer with an account of his first sexual stirrings at the age of seven, the contrast is explicit; in the second half of the poem, by an abrupt transition, we are given a view of recurring human destiny in the figure of Phlebas the Phoenician. The passage has great evocative power, and Eliot redrafted it in English and put it to stand alone as section four of *The Waste Land* under the title 'Death by Water':

Dans le Restaurant, extract

Phlébas, le Phénicien, pendant quinze jours noyé,
Oubliait les cris des mouettes et la houle de Cornouaille,
Et les profits et les pertes, et la cargaison d'étain:
Un courant de sous-mer l'emporta très loin,
Le repassant aux étapes de sa vie antérieure.

Figurez-vous donc, c'était un sort pénible;
Cependant, ce fut jadis un bel homme, de haute taille.

The Waste Land, IV. Death by Water
Phlebas the Phoenician, a fortnight dead,
Forgot the cry of gulls, and the deep sea swell
And the profit and loss.
                    A current under sea
Picked his bones in whispers. As he rose and fell
He passed the stages of his age and youth
Entering the whirlpool.
                    Gentile or Jew
O you who turn the wheel and look to windward,
Consider Phlebas, who was once handsome and
    tall as you.

Eliot is here doing what George did: translating and adapting a poem previously written in French and building it into the structure of a major work in his mother tongue. Some indeed have thought that in this practice piece we have one of the germs of the larger poem, 'an earlier exploration of the vein of thought and feeling that is plumbed in *The Waste Land*'.[4] As George (or his spokesman) observed, the sounds join together in the poet's mind in a similar way in the foreign language to the way they do in his own, and so do the images and symbols. Phlebas is a symbol, not restricted to the sphere of one language rather than another. Here perhaps we have a case of one of Altenberg's five-finger exercises suddenly acquiring 'soul'.

Eliot's *Waste Land* and Pound's *Cantos* are polyglot poems in varying degrees. The most polyglot poems known to me are however written in prose. They are *Ulysses* and *Finnegans Wake*. In either of these works, but of course especially in *Finnegans Wake*, a word or a phrase may be like a stone thrown into a pool, which produces ever-widening ripples of association. It is Joyce's way of grappling with the deep-seated mistrust of all language as a means of precise expression which we saw shared by Hofmannsthal and Rilke, but also by Eliot, who expressed in a late poem one of the basic experiences of his generation—and Joyce's:

>   Words strain,
> Crack and sometimes break, under the burden,
> Under the tension, slip, slide, perish,
> Decay with imprecision, will not stay in place,
> Will not stay still.
>   (*Burnt Norton* V)

Joyce attempts to overcome this disadvantage by constructing an immensely flexible web of interwoven multiple associations, in which the very imprecision of words becomes an advantage. It does not matter if the words 'strain, crack and sometimes break [. . .] under the tension', because out of the fragments other words can be made or invented, and this becomes much easier if the writer is not limited to the resources of one language only. Joyce spent most of his life on the continent, in Trieste, Zürich and finally in Paris. He was a fluent speaker of several foreign languages and a passionate student of language in general. With this equipment he set out to rejuvenate English as an artistic medium, in which words could be made polyglot and polyvalent —polyvalent because polyglot.

At this point I ought to give a detailed interpretation of a passage from *Finnegans Wake* to demonstrate what I mean. I shall not do this, for two reasons. One is that I am not competent (the study of Joyce is a highly specialized branch of scholarship, especially in America); the other is that it would take far too long. I must restrict myself to two small examples. One of the chief figures in the book is H. C. Earwicker, whose name suggests the word 'earwig'; the French for 'earwig' is 'perce-oreille'; there is also a figure called Peirsse O'Reilly, who represents another aspect of Earwicker.[5] This is a fairly simple case. The second is more complicated, involving Joyce's study of the Koran. 'All the suras except the ninth', J. S. Atherton explains, 'begin with the formula known as the *Bismillah*: "In the name of Allah, the Merciful, the Compassionate".' Joyce starts a chapter in *Finnegans Wake* with the words: 'In the name of Annah the Allmaziful'. In the book the female protagonist of Earwicker is Anna Livia Plurabelle, who symbolises the river Liffey, on which Dublin stands, and it is clear that she is being called upon at this point. But *ana* is Turkish for 'mother', *mazi* is Turkish for 'olden times'. Thus Anna Livia is being invoked in a sacred formula as a primeval mother, which indeed is one of her functions in the book.[6]

Both these cases are examples of a device Joyce uses to achieve multiple associations—the polyglot pun. To most of his readers it seems extremely artificial and contrived. Psychoanalysts however have long known that the polyglot pun is one of the ways by which the unconscious expresses itself in dreams. An analyst working in Tel Aviv[7] reported that one of his patients dreamt that mice were rummaging in his body; he elucidated the dream as meaning pangs of conscience. Mice are rodents or gnawing animals; in Russian (one of the languages the patient knew) *ugryzenia sovesti* is the gnawing of conscience, in Hebrew (the vehicular language in Tel Aviv and the one in which the analysis was conducted) *mussar klajoth* is 'conscience in the bowels'. Both terms mean 'pangs of conscience', and we may probably add German *Gewissensbisse*, the bites of conscience. By a combination of these elements the gnawing animals invade the bowels as in the patient's dream. There is no suggestion that this is an abnormal phenomenon; on the contrary. Joyce in *Finnegans Wake* is dealing with subconscious and unconscious levels of existence, and especially with dreams. The device he uses is thus entirely appropriate. Nor is it as unusual in everyday life as one might think. Here in New Zealand I have seen a riverside cottage called *Waiwhare*— a pun on English 'Why worry?' and the Maori words for 'running water' and 'house' (though it seems that for them to be good Maori the elements should be reversed). This is an excellent example of a Joycean pun expressing on one level the situation of the house by the water and on the other the philosophy of its owner. I understand that very profound and esoteric bilingual puns are common in certain Oriental literatures, especially in Persian and Urdu, the second language in each case being Arabic, the sacred language of the Koran. European writers have been extremely reluctant to use them for serious purposes; doubtless because they felt that the element of incongruity in them was more suitable for wit or humour. Though wit and humour are present in abundance in *Finnegans Wake*, Joyce's use of the bilingual or multilingual pun goes far beyond that. In this respect his originality is obvious. Stuart Gilbert suggested as early as 1929, when only fragments of the work were available (it was not completed until 1939) that *Finnegans Wake* might well 'be easier reading for a polyglot foreigner than for an Englishman with but his mother-tongue'.[8]

Joyce's polyglot contemporaries were more concerned to keep the languages distinct; this is valid even for Eliot and Pound, and I would like to examine other cases of this kind before proceeding to more Joycean developments. I shall be concerned with members of the generation which grew up in Alsace and Lorraine just before the First World War. It was a distinguished generation, and its best-known representative is the Nobel Prizewinner Albert Schweitzer, himself a notable polyglot. Both provinces belonged to Germany, though many of their inhabitants spoke French. This generation produced four important poets—Yvan Goll, Hans Arp,

Ernst Stadler and René Schickele. Growing up in these frontier provinces they all aimed at producing a climate of the mind which should be European rather than French or German, international rather than national. This was at a time when chauvinism was rampant on both sides of the frontier on which they lived. The war of 1914 was a disastrous set-back, and Ernst Stadler was killed in action in the first months. The others, Goll, Arp, and Schickele, retired to safety in neutral Switzerland, where Goll and Arp knew Joyce in Zürich.

Goll came from Lorraine. The language of his childhood was French, but in pre-1914 Alsace-Lorraine the language of education and culture was German, and his first works were written in German. Rilke thought of himself as rootless, sometimes anxiously, sometimes proudly. Goll wrote of himself in 1919; 'Iwan Goll has no country; by destiny a Jew, by chance born in France, classed as a German by a rubber-stamped piece of paper'—'Iwan Goll hat keine Heimat: durch Schicksal Jude, durch Zufall in Frankreich geboren, durch ein Stempelpapier als Deutscher bezeichnet.'[9] Iwan Goll has no country—here already is a premonition of his great cycle of fifty-nine poems, *Jean sans Terre*, written between 1936 and 1944.

Goll, doubly homeless in the post-1919 world as Lorrainer and as Jew, *made* himself at home on both sides of the shifting national frontier. He first appears associated with the German expressionists, filled like them with a generous but rather starry-eyed ideal of the brotherhood of man which expressed itself in well-intentioned but often windy rhetoric. Below the rhetoric can be discerned the elements in which Goll really thinks—he thinks in images. Later he became associated with the surrealists in France, whose work with images was congenial to him, and he began to write in French. As his basic means of expression lay below the threshold of language, he was able to formulate it either in French or in German, or indeed, after his emigration to the United States in 1940, even with some degree of success in English. His world is surreal, but it is not private in the sense that Rilke's was. He espoused generous causes, his allegiance was to humanity rather than to France or Germany, to Frenchmen or Germans, and his poetry moved in a realm of the spirit common to both. His choice of German or French seems to have been conditioned largely by external circumstances; when he went to live in France after 1919 he wrote in French, though there is a steady trickle of verse in German throughout this period, and his published letters to his wife, who is bilingual, as he was himself, are almost invariably in German.[10] His major novels and other prose works are in French; his plays and one of his novels are in German; he frequently translated his plays and his essays—but only rarely his poetry—from one language into another. His great lyric cycle, *Jean sans Terre*, is in French, though some poems in it were first written in German. His reputation as a lyric poet rests largely on his work in French, yet in his last months in the Strasbourg hospital where he lay dying of leukaemia he returned to German and wrote the superb cycle *Traumkraut*. The two languages seem to have been for him simply alternative vehicles for the images which welled out of him, and I cannot agree with the rather romantically expressed views of critics (mainly writing in French) that he did not 'possess' the German and French languages but was 'possessed by' them.[11] He was, it seems, a man who lived not in one language *or* the other, but indifferently in both. In both languages he was conscious of the literary traditions which determined what could and could not be done with them. He never mixes them. He does not approach either of them as Rilke approached French—as a new instrument, without prejudice or history. In Rilke's French poems I feel no depth of tradition; the whole of French literature—apart from Paul Valéry—counts for nothing; he writes as though he were writing in Esperanto. Goll's use of both languages is rooted in the literary soil appropriate to each.

His one major poem in English is clearly of a different kind. He does not turn to English as Rilke turned to French, because the words were fresh and had no complicating associations for him. He writes in English for purely external reasons: because he wants to communicate with an English-speaking public in America. And so, after the bombing of Hiroshima and Nagasaki he wrote *Atom Elegy*: it is a heroic effort, but it is a failure, and he seems to have known it.[12]

> The Divine Garment clothed my blandished thighs
> Against the holy beasts and the mad angels
>   And the 10 numbers sprang from Adam's forehead
> The spheric fruit of the Sephirot
> Became the emblems of his crown
>   The cipher: birthplace of the sphinx
> Memorial of prenatal dawns
>   Past Delphi's tripod and cathedral domes
> Pythagoras' revolving harmonies
> Past Bruno's pyre and Einstein's time

Riding the wheel
The 10 again in sweet uranium 235
The seven-colored ray
Bursting from dying Self
The Infinite raped in Alamogordo.

Of the six poems which the cycle comprises, the last slips back into French. This circumstance illustrates the tension between communication and expression in Goll. Hermetic though his diction often is, his aim is not expression for its own sake, a purely personal and therefore self-centred utterance: he expresses in order to communicate and he does not greatly care which language he uses, provided that communication is established. He finds that his linguistic resources in the third language are not sufficient, so he gives it up. Goll is that rare thing, a truly equi-lingual poet. Precisely this has resulted in the chaotic condition of his accessible work. His widow and her associates are evidently determined to ensure that he is accepted as a major German poet in Germany and a major French poet in France. Thus editions of his French poems include versions of his German poems, usually from the hand of his widow; and editions of his German poems similarly include versions of his French poems, by various hands, that of his widow included.[13] The result is that a great deal of detailed research is sometimes necessary in order to make certain in which language Goll originally wrote any one poem. Distressing though this may be for the scholar, the success of this procedure on both sides of the Rhine indicates that Goll's message is in fact independent of the language it is written in. But I cannot help thinking that though it would doubtless please him to be thought of as a French poet in France and a German poet in Germany, he would have much preferred his work to be published in such a way that he would be seen to be what he is: a major European poet writing indifferently in German and French.

At one period of his life Goll, as the representative of the Rhein Verlag of Zürich, had extensive dealings with Joyce about the German translation of *Ulysses* which the firm published in 1927, and he worked on a German version of *Anna Livia Plura-belle*. He does not however achieve a mention, as far as I have been able to find out, in *Finnegans Wake*, perhaps because Joyce, though admitting that Goll was 'a poet of sorts', thought an article Goll had written about him 'rubbishy'.[14] By contrast, Goll's fellow-countryman Hans Arp has been immortalized in this way.

Arp's background is similar to Goll's, for he was an Alsatian equally at home in German and French. Like Goll, he began with German and later went over to French, returning to German towards the end of his life. Whatever the language of the home, German was the language of the school, of education and culture, and René Schickele, another Alsatian of the same generation, who, like Goll, spoke French at home, has described how rapidly he and others like him moved over from one language to the other.[15] Many of Arp's poems exist in parallel French and German versions, and it is often difficult to decide on the face of it which version came first (though Madame Arp tells me that she has no difficulty at all). But Arp's use of different languages is only one aspect of his total artistic personality. Important though he is as a poet, it is as a plastic artist that he has done his most distinguished work. The parallel between the use of different languages and the use of different media in the plastic arts is particularly clear in his case. Until his death in 1966 Arp was one of the grand old men of European art, beside Picasso and Kokoschka; only Picasso surpasses him in creativity and versatility. He was active as a painter, as a sculptor in the round, in the disposition of objects in relief on a flat surface, and in collage; he worked therefore in a wide variety of artistic media, and it is interesting to see the number of times he repeats the same piece of sculpture in different materials—first in bronze, then in one kind of stone, then in another kind of stone. So too with many of his poems—first in German, then in French, or vice versa. For him, as for the medieval and renaissance poet, language is simply material. It is not even necessarily a means of communication, as it was for Rilke, for Goll and even for Joyce.

This becomes clear when we consider his early years and the beginnings of Dada in Zürich in 1916. Here we have Arp, a bilingual Alsatian; three Germans, Richard Huelsenbeck, Hugo Ball and Emmy Hennings; and two Rumanians, Marcel Janco and Tristan Tzara, one of whom, Tzara, had a fair knowledge of French but a very imperfect knowledge of German, and had already written poetry in Rumanian before coming to Zürich. It was against this background that the sound poem became the lowest common denominator of the linguistic resources of the group. The sound poem had already been discovered in Russia by the Futurists, especially by Alexei Kručonnych, and news of it may have come through the painter Kandinsky, whom Arp and Ball had visited in Munich before the war and who was in touch with the latest developments in Russia.[16] Kručonnych had elaborated *zaumnyi jazyk* or transrational language; for him it was 'the creation, from existing phonemes, of absolutely meaningless combinations in order to obtain freedom from meaning'.[17] Kandinsky himself had written, in *Über das Geistige in der Kunst* (1912), referring to the repetition of words until they become empty of meaning; 'Pure sound exercises a direct impression on the soul. The soul attains to an objectless vibration, even more complicated, I might say more transcendent, than the reverberations released by the sound of a bell, a stringed instrument, a fallen board. In this direction lie great possibilities for the literature of the future.'[18] Kandinsky himself had a good knowledge of German and wrote poetry in it; the title of his volume of poems, *Klänge (Sounds, 1912)*, which Arp greatly admired, suggests that he was following up his theoretical realization, but the poems themselves do not confirm it.

Sound poems in this sense were rediscovered by the Dadaists in Zürich, where they were felt to be particularly appropriate for reasons stated. They also practised—and probably invented—the simultaneous poem and the polyglot co-operative poem. This last was the result of a sort of game of 'consequences' or 'Heads Bodies and Legs' played by two or more people, each contributing lines in different languages. A pleasing example by Arp and Tzara is this:[19]

> *Balsam cartouche*
> Kocht der Adam seine maus zu mus
> blättern leicht steinvögler in granit
> kratzt das milde gnu die geigennuss
> le gendarme amour qui pisse si vite.
>   wattehufe tragen dornenmann
> esel treibt in sonnenschwamm am tor
> coq et glace se couchent sous l'œil galant
> träumern kommt der cactus seltsam vor.
>   grande lampe est claire vierge marie
> wassersattel trägt den schatten fort
> rue saint jacques s'en vont les petits jolis
> vers les timbres de l'aurore marine morte
>   purgatoire annonce la grande saison
> hat sie je mit katzenleim gebuhlt
> l'eau du diable pleure sur ta raison
> pfau und stern signieren 'katapult'.

Here the immediate object is not communication, but exploration of the expressive resources of language at a deep, subconscious,

magical level. Arp's own poetry at this time is not designed to
extend the way in which language can be made to *express*, but to
explore what it can be made to *do*. Hence his 'Wortokulierungen',
word-graftings, arising out of the pun, the portmanteau-word,
and the use of distorted spellings. This naturally interested Joyce
and his friends, and it was this side of Arp's art which they
remembered. Eugène Jolas—like Goll a bilingual Lorrainer by
origin, but American by upbringing—pointed to Arp as a fore-
runner of Joyce's word-play in 1929, saying that he 'played havoc
with the lyric mind by inventing word combinations set against
a fantastic ideology'.[20] It was presumably this aspect which induced Joyce to immortalize Arp in *Finnegans Wake* in the following characteristically multivalent sentence: 'Both were white in
black arpists at cloever spilling, knickt?' [508.33].

Atherton[21] sees here a reference to the white and black arts and
magic spells, brought into connexion with 'the humbler art of
spelling. There is also,' he goes on to say, 'someone playing
(German *spielen* to play or perform) upon a harp. Hans Arp
and his clever spelling are however the basis of the complex
structure. It is the distortion of the spelling of "clever" which
brings in most of the extra meanings, for there is a multilingual
pun on clover, *Klee, clef*, key, that ties up with a whole group
of references to shamrock and clover,' and with the artist Paul
Klee, whom Joyce and Arp both admired. (There seems to be
no foundation for Atherton's strange assertion that 'Arp was
for a time the publicity agent for Klee and the Dadaists'.) We
can however find more in it. 'White in black arpists' refers to
the title of Arp's volume of poetry *Weisst du schwarzt du*, which
puns on the verb *wissen, ich weiss, du weisst*, 'to know', and the
homophone *weiss* 'white' with its contrary, *schwarz*, 'black', in a
way that would appeal to Joyce. The clover can also refer to
German *Kleeblatt*, 'clover leaf', which is often used to designate
a trio of friends, here possibly Arp, Ball and Tzara, the principal
figures of the Dadaist group in Zürich when Joyce was there.
The French homophone of *Klee, la clef* 'the key', suggests on the
one hand the importance of Klee's ideas for Joyce's work, to
which, as Atherton has shown, they are one of the keys, and on
the other hand that Arp's deformation of language is a key to
Joyce's technique. 'Knickt?' with the question-mark is clearly the
German interrogative 'nicht?' at the end of a sentence, but the
'clever spelling' with *k* suggests an association with English *know*
if we take the *k* to be silent, as the association with 'nicht' requires,

referring back to 'weisst du' in the title of Arp's book, while if we
pronounce the *k* we get the third person singular present indi-
cative of the German verb *knicken* to bend or break, referring to
Arp's treatment of language.

The title *Weisst du schwarzt du* is characteristic and has proved
the efficacy of this playing with language because people have
remembered it, especially since Joyce's massive use of the same
technique, and have somehow gained the impression that all of
Arp's poetry is like that. Jolas, who published poetry by Arp
in his international avantgarde journal *transition,* still thought so
in 1929, as we have seen. In fact it is a stage that Arp soon
grew out of; by the time he went over to French he had got
beyond it, and there are few word-grafts in his French poems.
This again is nothing to do with the Genius of the French Language; it is a function of Arp's own development. French literature has its own notable word-grafters—Léon-Paul Fargue,
Jacques Prévert, and in his very different way Henri Michaux, to
say nothing of Rabelais. Arp found word-grafting ultimately un-
satisfying for two reasons: first, because its poetic resources were
soon explored, unless one takes it to the lengths Joyce did but
which Arp apparently either never envisaged or did not find
congenial (though it can remain an amusing parlour-game); and
secondly, because he was becoming aware that the basic material
with which he had really been working all the time was not
words at all but images, and, deeper than that, with patterns.[22]
Arp is really concerned with making satisfying patterns with
shapes, with colours, with poetic images, and—if need be—with
words. With this range of material available to him he found
that the resources of words, taken by themselves, not as the
vehicle of a poetic image, were soon exhausted; for Joyce, words
were the only medium he could use, so he concentrated on them.

Arp calls many of his sculptures 'concretions'; they are concrete in the sense that they are three-dimensional, that they exist
in space and you can stand in front of them or walk round them
or hold them in your hand; they are also con-crete in the sense
that they are the result of an organic creative patterning process
of 'growing together'. They have their own existence which we
must accept, and we must understand them on their own terms.
So too with his poems, and many of them refer directly or
obliquely to other works of his in painting, or more usually in
sculpture. I have indicated elsewhere[23] how the figure of Kaspar,
who appears in one of Arp's best known early poems, *Weh unser*

guter Kaspar ist tot, continually reappears in his sculpture. The poem exists in a number of different versions in German; Kaspar is a concretization of some thing or things which have occupied Arp throughout his life, to which he has given form, not only in language, but in other different artistic media—bronze, alabaster, granite. Arp's image patterns are thus not bound up with specific unique formulations in words; they can be stated or re-stated in any medium or in any language, and this in fact is what he often does.[24] In so far as he plays with words and their associations, the result is often different in the French and German versions of a poem, because the different words in the two languages give rise to different chains of association, but behind them there is usually an image-cluster or some determining pattern. For instance, in a nonsense poem which exists in both languages[25] the German line occurs: 'eine tabakspfeife auf puppenfüssen' (a tobacco-pipe on doll's feet); the corresponding French line is: 'une pipe à papa sur des pieds de poupée'. The rhythm and alliteration in French are much richer than in German, and they suggest that the poem was originally composed in French; this supposition is strengthened by the circumstance that the poem begins:

deux petits arabes adultes et arabesques
qui jouaient sur deux petits violons d'ingres
se promenaient dans les rides de deux petits violons runiques
lorsqu'une pipe surgit brusquement
devant les deux petits arabes adultes et arabesques
une pipe à papa sur des pieds de poupée [. . .]

zwei kleine erwachsene arabeskenaraber
spielten auf zwei kleinen steckenpferdgeigen
plötzlich tauchte eine tabakspfeife
vor den kleinen erwachsenen arabeskenarabern auf
eine tabakspfeife auf puppenfüssen [. . .]

Violon d'Ingres is the French term for a hobby; there is no corresponding German term involving a musical instrument, so Arp invents the compound *steckenpferdgeige,* which is a neat nonsense-translation but lacks the immediacy and the wit of the French. Even so, it would I think be a mistake to assume that the French text is therefore more authentic. In view of the number of different revisions of individual poems, many of which Arp prints side by side in his collected German poems and thus evidently considers equally valid,[26] there is no reason to suppose that his versions in different languages of the same poem are not just as authentic. It therefore seems unlikely, as Reinhard Döhl points out, that it will ever be possible to produce a definitive edition of Arp's poetry, at least with the traditional editorial techniques.

As long as poetry was regarded in the romantic mode as primarily expressing the inner life of the poet, and as long as languages were regarded in the same mode as having their own unique characteristics, soul or spirit, the poet's inner life was so bound up with the spirit of the language in which he had first learnt to express himself that potentially bilingual or polyglot poets tended to restrict themselves to the use of one language only, which they espoused as a conscious or half-conscious act of allegiance. Those poets who, like George, used foreign languages for workshop practice tended to keep the result unpublished. Even poets who, just before and just after World War I, had stood for a European cultural community like the Alsatians and Lorrainers Stadler, Schickele, Jolas, bilingual though they were, usually restricted themselves to the use of one language. This is why Goll is such a rare phenomenon. The Dadaists, with their attack on language as a vehicle of communication, of conventional sense, again made it possible for individual languages to be used as raw material, though in a different way from the way they had been used in the Middle Ages. But Dada also made it possible for the Rumanians Tristan Tzara and Eugène Ionesco and the Irishman Samuel Beckett to feel at liberty to write in French if they wished to, without necessarily burdening themselves with guilt-feelings. Beckett has always neatly sidestepped the question of why he writes in French, as in his answer to the Swiss critic Nikolaus Gessner—'Parce qu'en français c'est plus facile d'écrire sans style.' But he seems to have got close to an answer in reply to an American journalist, Israel Shenker, in 1956, when he said: 'It was a different experience from writing in English. It was more exciting for me, writing in French.'[27] The unromantic explanation is convincing in its simplicity. It is the way a sculptor might speak of working in wood after a long period of working in stone. It is paralleled by that of the contemporary Dutch poet Leo Vroman, who is engaged in medical research work in New York and who writes in English as well as in Dutch. His reply to a similar question by a Dutch critic was that he sometimes wrote poems in English because it was fun.[28] It is hard to imagine this uncomplicated approach before 1916, when Dada was launched. Even so, the romantic attitude is not entirely superseded. Many English readers feel that it is perverse and somehow disloyal of Beckett to write in French, even though he has not ceased writing in English. Joyce did at least pretend to write in English; Beckett

does not even pretend. For Beckett as for Vroman the foreign
language is just another medium.

Stefan George used an invented language for workshop practice.
Many people have invented private languages, usually as a secret
means of communication or as a kind of personal cypher. In *The
Lord of the Rings* J. R. R. Tolkien uses a number of invented
languages and has included some fine poetry written in them. His
is quite a different case; the languages came first and everything
else followed. Tolkien tells me that he long ago invented some
languages out of pure philological enthusiasm; as they seemed to
work, he thought it would be interesting to invent people who
spoke them. The result was the whole thrilling world of dwarves,
elves and hobbits which is already being exploited for Ph.D theses
by the academic machine, mainly in the United States.

In recent years literary experimentation with language has taken
a quite different course. Concrete poets now attempt to combine
visual image with poetic image by using, for instance, the sort of
typographical arrangement employed by Guillaume Apollinaire.
The image can be very simple; it may be evoked by one word only.
The language used is therefore of secondary importance, and may
even be determined by the extent to which certain words can be
exploited—either typographically or soundwise. Thus the French
word *soleil* would offer more possibilities than the English word
sun, not least because it contains the letter *o* which can be arranged
typographically to symbolise the sun; the French word *sol* meaning
'ground, earth'; and even the French word *œil* meaning 'eye'; by
clever typographical arrangement the word can be so displayed as
to suggest the sun as an eye looking down on the earth. A poet
can even write a concrete poem in a language of which he is ignor-
ant. The English poet Bob Cobbing has done this, taking as basic
text some words in a South American Indian language which he
found in a book, and imposing a rhythmic pattern on them. This
is a further development of the Dadaist and Futurist 'sound poem'.[29]

Concrete poetry has become a world-wide movement in the last
ten years, and the juggling with sounds, letters and shapes gives
rein to the deep-seated play-urge which we all possess.[30] The result
is a truly international poetic idiom, and it is worth noting that
many of the pioneers of concrete poetry are polyglot by upbringing
or environment. This is true of Eugen Gomringer, a Swiss born and
partly brought up in Bolivia, who is considered the founding
father of the movement, and who uses German, Spanish and
English.[31] Though not by any means all, or even most, concrete

poets are polyglot, many produce not only poems in different languages but also polyglot poems, or poems made of 'international' words.

As early as 1923 the pioneer Russian constructivist El Lissitzky produced a design with lettering in a form which comes very close to some modern concrete poetry in his *Der Sieg über die Sonne*. The lettering forms a short sentence containing elements of five languages—German, French, English, Russian and Italian. The Belgian concrete poet Paul de Vree combines English and Italian words in some of his Dutch poems, and he also writes in French. He uses sonorous proper names like *Veronica* and international words like *vertigo*.[32]

The sonority and the associative power of geographical and personal names have been exploited by poets for centuries, and Milton for instance made effective use of them in *Paradise Lost*. Names also form an international body of linguistic material and could thus be used as a basis for an international poetry. The Austrian composer Ernst Toch in fact produced a poem of this kind as early as 1930, using geographical names, in his *Geographical Fugue*.[33] It was not his intention to produce poetry at all, but to demonstrate that music could be written based on rhythm only without difference in pitch. He uses themes consisting of names with different rhythms—e.g. Honolulu, Mississippi, Titicaca; Canada, Mexico, Trinidad; Yókohama, Nágasaki; Tibet—spoken by four voices, soprano, alto, tenor and bass, and weaves them into a classical fugue form. It is spoken, not sung.

Whether he knew it or not, Toch was in fact elaborating on the 'simultaneous poem', a form invented by the Dadaists in 1916. They used three voices reciting nonsense texts in German, English and French. This has been further developed in the long polyphonic poem *Revenge* (1964)[34] by the English concrete poet Kenneth Robinson, who seems not to be aware of the work of the Dadaists or of Ernst Toch. In other ways too concrete poets are continuing Dada without being aware of it. In 1958 the American Brion Gysin could say, 'Writing is fifty years behind painting. I propose to apply the painter's techniques to writing: things as simple and immediate as collage or montage,' and go on to advocate cutting words out of a newspaper and shuffling them to obtain a text.[35] This is exactly what Arp was doing in the year Gysin was born, and André Breton and the Surrealists then carried it further.

The concrete poem can make very moving statements; many concrete poets are politically committed, especially in Brazil,[36] where they often aim at producing effective designs with words of a slogan type which can be easily understood by the public. One poem [37] of this kind is by two Czechs, Bohumila Grögerová and Josef Hiršal, which acquires additional poignancy in the light of recent events. I do not know whether it was originally planned as a committed poem or not when it was published in 1962. It represents a process of osmosis by which the Czech word for 'freedom' is gradually changed into the English one, aided by the circumstance that both have the same number of letters:

svoboda
vobodas
obodasv
bodasvo
odasvob
dasvobo
asvobod
fvoboda
vobodaf
obodafv
bodafvo
odafvob
dafvobo
afvobod
froboda
robodaf
obodafr
bodafro
odafrob
dafrobo
afrobod
freboda
rebodaf
ebodafr
bodafre
odafreb
dafrebo
afrebod
freeoda
reeodaf
eeodafr
eodafre
odafree
dafreeo
afreedo
freedom

'Osmosis' is the term used by the authors, and it is an interesting one because it is also used by Czech literary critics to describe the interaction between Czech and German literature in Prague in the early part of this century; it was the product of the symbiosis of Czech and German intellectuals, each knowing the other's language, which on the German side involved such major figures as Kafka, Rilke, Werfel and Max Brod; an aspect of polyglot literary life on which I can do no more than touch lightly here.[38]

One particular kind of polyglot poem has emerged from concrete poetry; it is the discovery of the Austrian poet Ernst Jandl, who in private life is a teacher of English at a large boys' school in Vienna, and who writes concrete poetry in both German and English. It is what he calls 'surface translation'. The art consists in rendering the sounds of a poem in one language by the nearest approximation to those sounds to be achieved by the use of *words* in the other language.[39] Jandl's prototype poem was his rendering of Wordsworth's 'My heart leaps up when I behold':

mai hart lieb zapfen eibe hold	My heart leaps up when I
er renn bohr in sees kai	behold
so was sieht wenn mai läuft	A rainbow in the sky;
begehen	So was it when my life began,
so es sieht nahe emma mähen	So is it now I am a man,
so biet wenn ärschel grollt	So be it when I shall grow old,
ohr leck mit ei!	Or let me die!
seht stein dies fader rosse	The child is father of the man,
mähen	And I could wish my days to
in teig kurt wisch mai desto	be
bier	Bound each to each by natural
baum deutsche deutsch	piety.
bajonett schur alp eiertier	

Jandl has described this technique to me as 'a means of writing poetry without initial ideas' (the English formulation is his own). Here too language is being treated as raw material, much as the sculptor treats clay. For the polyglot reader much of the charm arises from the surprising juxtapositions and surrealist images which are produced in this way, and not least from the exciting tension between the original and the 'translation'. Jandl himself seems not to view it in this light. For the translation to *sound* like the original, which for me is half the fun, it needs to be read very fast with a strong Viennese accent. There is a recording of him reading this poem, where he quite clearly avoids creating any

connexion with the English text in the mind of the listener; for
him it is simply a technical device for producing 'poetry without
initial ideas' in German. But we cannot forget that the starting
point is not German, and that the surface translation is one example
of polyglot poetry, though admittedly a special case. The element
of play is very strong, and if it is over-emphasized the surface
translation can easily become a parlour game (which I, and some
others, play with intense pleasure). As an example I would like
to cite a surface translation of a well-known poem by Rilke, composed in 1966 as a short collaborative effort over lunch by Ernst
Jandl, Christopher Middleton and myself:

Dare toadies gross	Der Tod ist gross.
Vere sinned designing	Wir sind die Seinen
Laugh in the moons.	lachenden Munds.
When we've ounce mitten	Wenn wir uns mitten im Leben
am lay-by mine in-	meinen
farct hair so whining	wagt er zu weinen
midden in noons.	mitten in uns.

The amusing books of Mr Afferbeck Lauder—e.g. *Let stalk Strine*
—are in principle doing much the same thing in a context of
diglossia, evidently under the influence of Joyce.[40] The parlour
game aspect is very clear here. So it is in the work of an ingenious
American writing under the name of Luis d'Antin Van Rooten,
who discovered the surface translation of poetry independently
of Jandl and apparently at much the same time. In his *Mots
d'heures, gousses, rames* (New York 1967) he made surface translations of *Mother Goose's Rhymes* into French, treated the result
as an ancient manuscript and added a body of playful learned
annotation:

> (*Humpty Dumpty sat on a wall*)
> Un petit d'un petit
> S'étonne aux Halles
> Un petit d'un petit
> Ah! Degrés te fallent
> Indolent qui ne sort cesse
> Indolent qui ne se mène
> Qu'importe un petit d'un petit
> Tout Gai de Raguennes.

His work is an elaborate academic joke, and a very good one;
Jandl's is a serious attempt at exploring the resources of the
German language. But Jandl, having shown that it can be done,
that it is a viable method of producing concrete poetry, has under-

standably lost interest and gone on to something else, which does
not concern us here.

The means employed by concrete poets, the radical dissociation
of sound and sense and the rearrangement of words in space to
produce new sense by juxtaposition, are not just a game, though
as we we have seen the play element is important and attractive.
They are also ways towards purification and repristination of
poetic diction. There are too many dirty words. Just how many
words are dirty nowadays is made clear by Shelley Berman's
Cleans and Dirties, which is not only a piece of entertainment but
a valuable collection of material in sociolinguistics. He comes to
the conclusion that 'no word, no thought, no object uttered in an
American frame of reference is inviolate'.[41] Words become dirty
because of their associations and the contexts in which they are
used. If they can be placed in other, not necessarily directly meaningful, contexts they may be made clean again. Poets need to
operate with clean words.

We have seen how important the use of foreign languages has
been for some modern poets in just this respect.[42] But concrete
poetry is also an extreme example of the use of language as
material, and a rather less extreme case of the creation of an
international poetic idiom irrespective of the language used. In
both respects it is close to medieval, renaissance and baroque
poetry. We have in fact been following a sort of spiral development after the manner of Vico—one of the great inspirers of
James Joyce—and we are back at the point from which we started,
though at a different level.

Much of what I have had to say can be summed up by a poem
by the Scot Hugh MacDiarmid, *The Caledonian Antisyzygy*:[43]

> I write now in English and now in Scots
> To the despair of friends who plead
> For consistency; sometimes achieve the true lyric cry,
> Next but chopped-up prose; and write whiles
> In traditional forms, next in a mixture of styles.
> So divided against myself, they ask:
> How can I stand (or they understand) indeed?
>
> Fatal division in my thought they think
> Who forget that although the thrush
> Is more cheerful and constant, the lark
> More continuous and celestial, and, after all,
> The irritating cuckoo unique
> In singing a true musical interval,

Yet the nightingale remains supreme,
The nightingale whose thin high call
And that deep throb,
Which seem to come from different birds
In different places, find an emotion
And vibrate in the memory as the song
Of no other bird—not even
the love-note of the curlew—
Can do!

1. Hugh Kenner, *The Poetry of Ezra Pound*, London 1951, p. 186.
2. Ibid., p. 215.
3. E. J. H. Greene, *T. S. Eliot et la France*, Paris n.d., p. 82 ff.
4. George Williamson, *A Reader's Guide to T. S. Eliot: a Poem-by-Poem Analysis*, 2nd ed., New York 1966, p. 118.
5. Samuel Beckett and others, *Our Exagmination round his Factification for Incamination of 'Work in Progress'*, Paris 1929, p. 159.
6. J. S. Atherton, *The Books at the Wake*, London 1959, p. 204 ff.
7. Immanuel Velikovsky, 'Can a newly acquired Language become the Speech of the Unconscious? Word-plays in the Dreams of Hebrew-thinking Persons', *Psychoanalytic Review* XXI (1934) p. 329 ff.
8. S. Beckett etc., *Our Exagmination*, p. 58.
9. Kurt Pinthus, ed., *Menschheitsdämmerung*, Berlin 1920, p. 292.
10. Iwan Goll-Claire Goll, *Briefe, mit einem Vorwort von Kasimir Edschmid*, Mainz 1966.
11. *Yvan Goll: quatre études par Jules Romains, Marcel Brion, Francis Carmody, Richard Exner; Œuvres choisies, facsimilés, portraits, dessins, inédits et documents, bibliographie* (= *Poètes d'aujourd'hui* 50), Paris 1956, p. 66. The observation is by Richard Exner, admittedly a German, but writing here for French readers. See also Marcel Brion, ib., pp. 15-16.
12. Yvan Goll, *Dichtungen: Lyrik Prosa Drama*, ed. Claire Goll, Neuwied-Berlin 1960, p. 799.
13. See the German edition cited in note 12 and the French in note 11.
14. James Joyce, *Letters*, ed. Stuart Gilbert and Richard Ellmann, London 1957 ff., III, p. 250.
15. René Schickele, *Werke*, Köln-Berlin 1959, III, pp. 784, 1155, 1200.
16. First pointed out by Raoul Hausmann, 'Introduction à une histoire du poème phonétique', *German Life and Letters* XIX (1965-6), p. 19 ff.
17. V. Markov, *The Longer Poems of V. Khlebnikov*, Berkeley 1962 (= *University of California Publications in Modern Philology* 62), p. 7.
18. Wassily Kandinsky, *Concerning the Spiritual in Art*, New York 1966 (= *The Documents of Modern Art* 5), p. 34. This edition also contains selected poems from *Klänge* in German with English translations.
19. Hans Arp, Richard Huelsenbeck, Tristan Tzara, *Die Geburt des Dada: Dichtung und Chronik der Gründer*, ed. Peter Schifferli, Zürich 1957, p. 95; see also Leonard Forster, *Poetry of Significant Nonsense*, Cambridge 1962, p. 29. For Tzara's early poetry in Rumanian see Claude Sernet, *Tristan Tzara, Les premiers poèmes, présentés et traduits du roumain*, Paris 1965.

20. S. Beckett etc., *Our Exagmination*, p. 86. On Jolas see Maria Jolas, 'Joyce's Friend Jolas' in M. Magalaner, ed., *A James Joyce Miscellany*, New York 1957, p. 62 ff.
21. Atherton, op. cit., p. 84.
22. This aspect of the creative process has yet to be fully explored. Fernande Saint-Martin, *La littérature et le non-verbal*, Montréal 1958, makes an unsatisfactory beginning, though she has interesting things to say about Dada, p. 101 ff. Arp's own lines are relevant here:
    la langue ne vaut rien pour parler
    pour parler servez-vous plutôt de vos pieds
    que de votre langue chauve
    pour parler servez-vous plutôt de votre nombril . . .
    Jean Arp, *Jours effeuillés*, Paris 1966, p. 156.
23. Leonard Forster, 'Un Wackes cosmique', *Saisons d'Alsace* XXII (1967) p. 209 ff., and *Cahiers Dada Surréalisme* II (1968), p. 25 ff. Herbert Read has a chapter on Arp's poetry in his *Arp*, London 1968, p. 139 ff. The most recent work is R. W. Last, *Hans Arp, the Poet of Dadaism*, London 1969.
24. Reinhard Döhl, *Das literarische Werk Hans Arps 1903-1930*, Stuttgart 1967, pp. 14 and 131 ff, with valuable bibliography.
25. The two texts are compared by Döhl, op. cit., p. 135 ff. Final versions in H. Arp, *Gesammelte Gedichte*, Wiesbaden 1963, p. 214 ff; *Jours effeuillés*, p. 244.
26. Döhl, op. cit., p. 146.
27. Both quoted by Ruby Cohen, *Samuel Beckett, the Comic Gamut*, Rutgers University Press 1962, p. 95. D. H. Curnow, 'Language and Theatre in Beckett's "English" Plays', *Mosaic* II (1968-69), p. 54 ff, sees a general distinction in Beckett's later work on the lines of 'English for theatre, French for literature'.
28. J. Bernlef and K. Schippers, *Wat zij bedoelen*, Amsterdam 1965, p. 70; previously in *De Gids*, 1965, p. 120 ff. Vroman includes English poems among his Dutch ones, but he has also published a volume of *Poems in English*, Amsterdam 1953.
29. Cobbing speaks this poem on *Writers Forum Record* 1, together with other sound poems based on French, German and Japanese. Further texts in Bob Cobbing, *Soundpoems*, Writers Forum Poets 7, London 1965. For an illuminating discussion of concrete poetry in general see Siegbert S. Prawer, 'Some Recent Language Games' in S. S. Prawer, R. Hinton Thomas and Leonard Forster, edd., *Essays in German Language, Culture and Society* (= *Publications of the Institute of Germanic Studies, University of London*, no. 12), London 1969. He deals with Cobbing on p. 73. Cobbing found the words in C. M. Bowra's *Primitive Song*, London 1962, pp. 58-61.
30. J. Huizinga, *Homo ludens, A Study of the Play-Element in Culture*, London 1949.
31. Emmett Williams, ed., *Anthology of Concrete Poetry*, © 1967 by Something Else Press, Inc., 276 Park Avenue South, New York, NY 10010. New York 1967, pp. iv and 334. The section of the book containing concrete poems is not paginated, but authors are arranged alphabetically.
32. Represented in Williams, *Anthology of Concrete Poetry;* see also *Form* 3 (1966), p. 23.
33. Ernst Toch, *Geographical Fugue*, Mills, New York 1960 (previously in *New Music* (XXIII) 1950). He also wrote a *Valse* on similar lines, New York 1962. See also *Grove's Dictionary of Music and Musicians*, 5th edn., ed. Eric Blom, London 1954, VIII, p. 487; *Die Musik in Geschichte und Gegenwart*, ed. F. Blume, Kassel 1949 ff, XIII, col.

444. A young German composer, Dieter Schnebel, has recently produced a work called *Glossolaly for an ensemble of speakers and in-
strumentalists*. 'This consists of meaningless fragments of speech from
30 languages and dialects, combined with the trilling of alarm signals on
pipes and other instruments' (*The Times*, Friday January 24 1969,
p. 12, col. 7). On the relation of glossolaly to certain aspects of modern
poetry see Forster, *Poetry of Significant Nonsense*, p. 36 ff. In this
connexion it is interesting to note that Schnebel is a Protestant pastor.

34. Kenneth Robinson, 'Polyphonic Poetry' (with an extract from
Revenge), *Form* 3 (1966), p. 24-5. For a dadaist 'poème simultané'
see Arp-Huelsenbeck-Tzara, *Die Geburt des Dada*, plate 6.

35. Brion Gysin, in Williams, *Anthology of Concrete Poetry*.

36. See the poems in Williams, *Anthology of Concrete Poetry*, by Augusto
and Haroldo de Campos, José Lino Grünewald and Décio Pignatari;
also Edwin Morgan's poem 'starryveldt', ibid.

37. Grögerová, in Williams, *Anthology of Concrete Poetry*. Reprinted by
permission.

38. Ludvík Václavek, 'Literaturen der kulturellen Vermittlung', *Philologica
Pragensia* XI (1967) p. 193 ff.

39. Ernst Jandl, *mai hart lieb zapfen eibe hold*, Writers Forum Poets no.
11, London 1965; *Laut und Luise*, Olten 1966. Jandl speaks his poetry
on *Writers Forum Record* 1 and *Wagenbachs Quartplatte* 2; Prawer,
op. cit., discusses Jandl's work on p. 74 ff. For a case of traditional
'folk' surface-translation from Welsh into English see Forster, *Poetry
of Significant Nonsense*, p. 6-7.

40. Afferbeck Lauder, *Let stalk Strine*, Sydney 1965; *Nose tone unturned*,
Sydney 1966; *Fraffly well spoken*, Sydney 1968.

41. Shelley Berman, *Cleans and Dirties*, Los Angeles 1966, Sydney and
London 1967, p. 13.

42. This is true too of the 'Babelian' group active in Montreal under the
aegis of Tristan Max Him (Henri Jones). Their manifesto stresses
that 'polylingualism does not only protect the freshness of the most
personal creation but also adapts itself to the deliriums of group work
and even to a highly elective communal life'. See also Tristan Max
Him, ed., *Babelian Illustrations* No. 1, Montreal 1969.

43. Hugh MacDiarmid, *Collected Poems*, London 1967, p. 477, by kind
permission of the author.

Index

Achebe, Chinua 5
Alba, Duke of 31
Alciati, Andrea 20, 21
Alewyn, Richard 49
Alfonso, King of Castile 16
Alsace 78
Altenberg, Peter 48, 50, 76
America 77, 80
Amsterdam 35, 38, 39
Andreas-Salomé, Lou 63, 64
d'Angennes, Julie 46
Antwerp 31, 32
Apollinaire, Guillaume 88
Arp, Hans 78, 79, 81, 82, 83, 84, 85, 87, 89, 94, 95, 96
Arp, Madame Hans 82
Atherton, J. S. 77, 84, 94, 95
Augsburg 20

Bachrach, A. G. H. 49
Ball, Hugo 84
Bangor 53
Barlaeus, Caspar 41, 42
Basel 24
Battersby, K. A. J. 72
Batts, Michael S. 24

Beatles, the 18
Beckett, Samuel 87, 88, 94, 95
Beckford, William 54
Beethoven, L. van 48
Berlin 58, 64
Berlitz School 2
Berman, Shelley 93, 96
Bernard, Tristan 13
Bernlef, J. 95
Bertini, Henri-Jerôme 48
Betjeman, John 42, 49
Béziers, M. 7
Bible 54
Blatt, F. 25
Blom, Eric 95
Blume, F. 95
Bock, C. V. 71
Böcking, E. 71
Bolivia 88
Bolte, Johannes 24
Boswell, James 52, 71
Bowra, C. M. 95
Brabant 35
Brazil 89
Bredero, Gerbrand Adriaensz 38, 49
Brenner, Albert 24

Breton, André 89
Bright, William 7
Brion, Marcel 94
Brod, Max 91
Bruder Hans 24
Brussels 58
Buitenen, J. A. B. van 24
Burger, Heinz Otto 48
Butler, E. M. 72

Cambridge 6, 16
Campbell, A. 25
Campen, Jacob van 41
Campos, Augusto de 96
Campos, Haroldo de 96
Canada 2
Carducci, Giosuè 51, 71
Carlyle, Thomas 54
Carmody, Francis 94
Carney, James 24
Cats, Jacob 20, 21, 25, 27, 37
Catullus 33
Chambers, E. K. 25
Chanson de Roland 74
Charles d'Orléans 19, 25
Charles V, Emperor 17, 25, 47
Chaytor, H. J. 16, 25
Cobbing, Bob 88, 95
Cohen, Ruby 95
Colie, Rosalie L. 49
Cologne 31, 32
Conrad, Joseph 55
Coulton, G. G. 9, 23
Curnow, D. H. 95
Curtius, Ernst Robert 20
Czerny, Carl 48

Dada 82, 83, 87, 88, 89, 94, 96
Dalhousie, Lord 52
Dante 75
Day, M. 25
De amico ad amicam 16, 17
De Heinrico 10
Denison, Norman 7
Diodati, G. 45
Döhl, Reinhard 86, 95
Dorsten, J. A. van 48
Dronke, Peter 24
Duarte, Francisca 41
Du Bartas, Guillaume 21, 25
Du Bellay, Joachim 30
Dublin 77
Du Bos, Charles 63, 72
Du Deffand, Mme 52, 71
Duthie, Enid Lowry 72

Edschmid, Kasimir 94
Eliot, T. S. 70, 74, 75, 76, 78, 94

Ellman, Richard 94
England 42, 52
'Ex!' 22, 23
Exner, Richard 94

Fabricius, Vincentius 35
Fargue, Léon-Paul 65, 85
Farrell, R. A. 62, 72
Favre, Mme Renée 72
Ferguson, Charles A. 8
Fischer, H. 48
Fishman, Joshua A. 7
Fletcher, C. R. L. 25
Flinn, John E. 49
Folengo, Teofilo 14, 15, 25
Forster, Leonard 24, 48, 49, 94, 95, 96
France 42, 69, 70, 79, 81
Frankfurt 58
Frederick the Great 52
Frederick Henry, Prince of Nassau 41
French Academy 54
Friedenthal, Richard 71
Froe, Balthasar 31

Gawen, Thomas 28, 37
Genthe, F. W. 25
George I, King of England 52
George, Stefan 56, 57, 58, 59, 60, 61, 62, 64, 70, 71, 74, 75, 76, 87, 88
Gérardy, Paul 60
Germany 14, 39, 42, 70, 78, 79, 81
Gessner, Nikolaus 87
Giauque, Sophie 72
Gilbert, Stuart 78, 94
Gilliat, Sidney 24
Gladding, E. B. 72
Glasenapp, Helmuth von 24
Glasgow 55
Godley, A. D. 15, 25
Goertz, Hartmann 72
Goethe, J. W. von 52, 54, 71
Goldsmith, Oliver 71
Goldsmith, Ulrich K. 71
Goll, Claire 94
Goll, Yvan 78, 79, 80, 81, 82, 87, 94
Gomez, E. García 24
Gomringer, Eugen 88
Gottsched, J. C. 44
Gower, John 16
Grace, Louisa 71
Gräf, Hans Gerhard 71
Grappe, Georges 73
Greek Anthology 20
Greene, E. J. H. 94
Grierson, Sir Herbert 49

INDEX

Griffith, Richard 24
Grillparzer, Franz 18, 25
Grimm, the Brothers 60
Grimm, Reinhold 48
Grimmelshausen, J. J. C. von 29
Grögerová, Bohumila 90, 96
Grünewald, José Lino 96
Gumperz, John J. 8
Gundolf, Friedrich 6
Gustavus Adolphus, King of Sweden 27
Gysin, Brion 89, 96

Hamburg 35
Hampton Court 43
Hanover 52
Harris, Clement 71
Haugen, Einar 7
Hausmann, Raoul 94
Hay, James 35
Heger, Klaus 24
Heinsius, Daniel 21
Henkel, A. 25
Hennings, Emmy 82
Henric van Veldeke 16
Henry II, King of France 28, 48
Herder, J. G. 54
Hessen, Landgraf Moritz von 27, 28
Him, Tristan Max (Henri Jones) 96
Hiroshima 80
Hiršal, Josef 90
Hocke, Gustav René 50
Hoffmann von Fallersleben, A. 24
Hofmannsthal, Hugo von 2, 7, 48, 50, 64, 76
Holland, 42, 53
Hollywood 18
Holstein, Anna Sabina, Duchess of 36
Homann, Holger 25
Hooft, P. C. 39, 40, 41, 46, 49
Horace 21, 22, 29
Huelsenbeck, Richard 82, 94, 96
Huizinga, J. 95
Huygens, Christiaan 41
Huygens, Constantijn 41, 42, 47, 49, 51
Hymes, Dell 7, 8

Ibsen, Henrik 56
In dulci jubilo 10
India 4
Ionesco, Eugène 87
Italy 4, 18, 75

Jaeger, Hans 59, 71, 72
James I, King of England 25, 36
Janco, Marcel 82

Jandl, Ernst 91, 92, 96
Janssens, W. 48
Johnson, Dr Samuel 52, 71
Jolas, Eugene 84, 85, 87, 95
Jolas, Maria 95
Jones, Henri 96
Joyce, James 75, 76, 77, 79, 81, 82, 84, 85, 87, 93, 94, 95
Julius Friedrich, Duke of Württemberg 35, 37

Kafka, Franz 90
Kalidasa 13
Kandinsky, Wassily 82, 83, 94
Kenner, Hugh 74, 94
Key, Ellen 72
Khlebnikov, V. 94
Klee, Paul 84
Klein, Carl August 59
Klein, K. K. 25
Knoop, Gertrud Ouckama 73
Knuttel, J. A. N. 49
Koestler, Arthur 55
Kohlschmidt, W. 25
Kokoschka, Oskar 82
Koran 77, 78
Korff, H. A. 6
Kortwich, Werner 24
Kracauer, Siegfried 24
Kruconnych, Alexei 82, 83
Kuhn, Hans 8

La Fontaine, Jean de 50
Laforgue, Jules 75
Lancaster, H. Carrington 49
Last, R. W. 95
Lauder, Afferbeck 92, 96
Leavis, F. R. 6
Leendertz, P. 49
Leibniz, G. W. 52
Leiden 38
Leipzig 52
Lind, Georg Rudolf 71
Lindtberg, Leopold 24
Linskill, Joseph 24, 25
Lissitzky, El 89
London 31
Lorraine 13, 78, 79, 84
Luke, David 71
Lund, Zacharias 38, 49
Luther, Martin 10, 23
Luxembourg, Maréchale de 54
Luzio, A. 25
Lydgate, John 16

MacDiarmid, Hugh 93, 96
McGill University 6
Mackey, W. F. 7, 8

Magalaner, M. 95
Mallarmé, Stéphane 59, 60
Maoris 4, 78
Margaret, Queen of Navarre 17
Marino, G. B. 51
Markov, V. 94
Mason, E. C. 68, 72, 73
Matthias, Thomas 71
Mazon, André 71
Ménage, Gilles 41, 49
Merrill, Stuart 59
Meyer, Conrad Ferdinand 55
Michaux, Henri 85
Middelburg 21
Middleton, Christopher 92
Milton, John 44, 45, 47, 49, 52, 75, 89
Mohr, Wolfgang 25
Moland, L. 49
Molière, J. B. 14, 41, 47, 49
Montcalm, General Louis Joseph de 52
Montreal 2, 3, 6, 96
Morax, René 73
Moréas, Jean 59
Morgan, Edwin 96
Morgan, J. A. 25
Moritz, Landgraf of Hessen 27, 28
Morwitz, Ernst 71
Moscow 63
Mourgues, Odette de 50
Muiden 39
Mulhouse 5
Munich 82
Muzot 65, 72

Nagasaki 80
Nassau, Prince Frederick Henry of 41
Nerval, Gérard de 75
New York 87
New Zealand 1, 6, 78
Newmarket 43
Nigeria 5
Noot, Jan van der 30, 31, 32, 33, 34, 35, 39, 40, 48, 49, 51
Nykl, A. R. 24

Oatlands 43
Odyssey 57
Opitz, Martin 32, 37, 44
Oswald von Wolkenstein 17, 25
Overbeke, M. van 7
Oxford 15, 18

Quebec 52

Pabst, G. W. 13
Palatine, Elector 36
Paris 53, 55, 58, 61, 77
Parker, A. G. 24
Paschal, Léon 60
Pervigilium Veneris 75
Pessoa, Fernando 71
Petrarch, F. 29, 46, 48
Picasso, Pablo 82
Pignatari, Décio 96
Pinthus, Kurt 94
Plains of Abraham 52
'Pléiade' 30
Pliny 20
Pound, Ezra 70, 74, 75, 76, 78, 94
Prague 91
Prawer, Siegbert S. 95, 96
Praz, Mario 25
Prévert, Jacques 85

Rabelais, François 85
Raimbaut de Vaqueiras 12, 24, 25
Rambouillet, Mme de 46, 49
Ramon Vidal de Besalú 16
Rassenfosse, Edmond 60
Read, Herbert 95
Renoir, Jean 13
Responcio 17
Rilke, R. M. 55, 62, 63, 64, 65, 66, 67, 68, 69, 70, 72, 73, 76, 79, 80, 82, 91, 92
Ristow, Brigitte 25
Robinson, Kenneth 89, 96
Rodin, Auguste 69, 73
Roggen, K. Graadt van 49
Romains, Jules 94
Ronsard, Pierre de 30, 32, 33, 34
Rossellini, Roberto 24
Rossetti, D. G. 62
Rotha, Paul 24
Russia 14, 52, 63, 64, 82, 83

Saint-Martin, Fernande 95
Saint-Paul, Albert 59
Sampson, Anthony 8
Sappho 33
Schazmann, P. E. 72
Scherer, Wilhelm 6
Schickele, René 55, 79, 82, 87, 94
Schifferli, Peter 94
Schiller, F. von 29, 30
Schippers, K. 95
Schlegel, August Wilhelm 54, 71
Schnebel, Dieter 95
Schonauer, Franz 71, 72
Schöne, Albrecht 25
Schurman, Anna Margarethe van 38
Schurman, Anna Maria van 38

Schweitzer, Albert 78
Scotland 6, 52
Scott, Cyril 58, 62, 72
Sén Dé 24
Sernet, Claude 94
Shakespeare, W. 13, 51
Shaw, Bernard 12
Shenker, Israel 87
Sidgwick, F. 25
Sidney, Sir Philip 30
Simon, Daniel 73
Smart, J. S. 50
Soloveitchik, Samson 72
Spencer, John 8
Spenser, Edmund 31, 51
Spiegels, Brechje 39, 49
Stadler, Ernst 79, 87
Staël, Mme de 54
Steele, R. 25
Stern, S. M. 12, 24
Stoett, F. A. 49
Stolt, Birgit 10, 23
Strachey, Lytton 54, 55, 71
Strasbourg 53, 80
Strich, Fritz 6
Stuttgart 35, 37
Suerbaum, Ulrich 71
Swinburne, A. C. 62
Switzerland 18, 22, 24, 69, 79
Sylvester, Joshua 21, 25

Tacitus 40
Tel Aviv 77, 78
Thomas, R. Hinton 95
Toch, Ernst 89, 95
Tolkien, J. R. R. 88
Tricht, H. W. van 49
Trieste 77
Trumbull, William 43
Tyler, Royall 25
Tzara, Tristan 82, 83, 87, 94, 96

United States of America 79, 88
Upanishads 75
Utenhove, Carolus 28, 30, 48
Utrecht 38

Václavek, Ludvik 96
Vaenius, Otto 21, 26
Valais, Canton 56, 65, 69, 73
Valéry, Paul 69, 70, 80
Van Rooten, Luis d'Antin 92

Velikovsky, Immanuel 94
Vico, G. B. 93
Viélé-Griffin, Francis 59
Vienna 91
Vildomec, Veroboj 7
Visscher, Maria Tesselschade 41, 49
Voiture, Vincent 41, 49
Vondel, Joost van den 38, 39, 41
Vree, Paul de 89
Vroman, Leo 87, 88, 95

Wales 6
Walpole, Horace 52, 53
Weckherlin Georg Rudolf 27, 35, 36,
    37, 41, 42, 43, 44, 45, 48, 49, 51,
    58
Weevers, Theodoor 49
Weidner, J. L. 27, 28
Weinhold, Karl 24
Weinreich, Uriel 5, 8, 25
Wellington, N.Z. 18
Werfel, Franz 91
Westminster Abbey 52
Whitehall 43
Wiedemann, Conrad 48
Wiese, Benno von 49
Wilde, Oscar 54
Williams, Emmet 95
Williams, Leonard Llewellyn Bulkeley
    55, 71
Williamson, George 94
Witstein, S. F. 49
Wodtke, F. W. 72
Wolfe, General James 52
Wordsworth, W. 91
Worp, J. A. 49
Wulf, Joseph 24
Württemberg, Duke Julius Friedrich
    of 35, 37

Zaalberg, C. A. 48, 49
Zealand 37
Zedlitz, G. W. von 18, 25
Zermatten, Maurice 72, 73
Zesen, Philip von 38, 42, 49
Zincgref, Julius Wilhelm 28
Zinn, Ernst 72
Zipper, Albert 25
Zissermann, N. 72
Zuckmayer, Carl 13
Zumthor, Paul 24
Zürich 77, 81, 82, 83, 84